365 DAYS OF INNER TRANSFORMATION

Nurturing your Mind, Body and Spirit

LYN M. KWENDA

MY BELOVED PARENTS NEVISON & PETINA KWENDA

Just thinking about you brings tears to my eyes, a smile to my face and the most thankful feeling I'll ever have in my heart.

Your unconditional love taught me to be able to forgive and detach peacefully.

You will forever remain in my heart. In the clouds, we will meet again. R.I.P.

ACKNOWLEDGMENT

I would like to express my heartfelt gratitude to everyone who has supported me throughout the journey of creating this devotional.

First and foremost, I thank God for guiding my thoughts and providing inspiration at every turn. My deepest appreciation goes to my family and friends, whose unwavering encouragement and love have been my constant source of strength.

A special thanks to my spiritual father, my pastor, Dr. Alph Lukau, for his invaluable wisdom and insights, which have shaped my understanding and deepened my faith. I am also grateful to the community members who shared their stories and experiences, reminding me of the beauty and power of shared faith.

Lastly, I want to acknowledge the readers of this devotional. Your openness and willingness to explore these reflections inspire me to continue writing and sharing. May this devotional serve as a light on your own spiritual journey.

Thank you all for being part of this endeavor.

Contents

INTRODUCTION

Welcome to "365 Days of Inner Transformation: Nurturing Your Mind, Body, and Spirit." This devotional journey is designed to guide you toward personal growth and holistic well-being by nurturing your mind, body, and spirit. Over the course of 365 days, we will explore various aspects of self-care, reflection, and spiritual nourishment, drawing inspiration from the wisdom of the Bible.

Each day, you will encounter a carefully selected Bible verse that relates to a specific theme, accompanied by a brief commentary to deepen your understanding and provide practical insights. Additionally, you will find a heartfelt prayer that invites you to connect with God, seek His guidance, and experience His transformative power in your life.

This devotional is an invitation to prioritize self-care and intentional reflection, recognizing that true transformation occurs when we nurture our minds, care for our bodies, and cultivate our spirits. It is an opportunity to deepen your relationship with God, grow in self-awareness, and embrace a holistic approach to your well-being.

As you embark on this 365-day journey, may you experience renewal, healing, and growth. May you be inspired to make positive changes, embrace gratitude, and align your life with God's purposes. May your mind, body, and spirit be nurtured, leading to a deeper sense of peace, joy, and wholeness. Open your heart to the transformation that awaits you, and let this devotional be a guide on your path to inner renewal.

May you be abundantly blessed as you embark on this journey of inner transformation.

Welcome and Purpose of the Devotional

Welcome to "365 Days of Inner Transformation: Nurturing Your Mind, Body, and Spirit." This devotional series is designed to provide you with a dedicated space and time to focus on your holistic well-being. In our fast-paced lives, it is easy to neglect self-care and overlook the importance of nurturing our minds, caring for our bodies, and cultivating our spirits.

The purpose of this devotional is to guide you on a transformative journey towards inner growth and renewal. Over the course of 365 days, you will explore various themes and practices that promote a balanced and thriving life. Through reflections, Bible verses, commentaries, and prayers, you will be encouraged to deepen your relationship with God, develop a greater understanding of yourself, and foster a sense of harmony and wholeness.

During this journey, you will be invited to engage in practices that nurture your mind, such as cultivating positive thoughts, renewing your mindset, and seeking wisdom from the Scriptures. You will also explore ways to care for your body, including physical exercises, healthy habits, and self-care routines. Additionally, you will be encouraged to cultivate your spirit through prayer, meditation, and embracing spiritual disciplines.

The purpose of this devotional is not just to provide information but to facilitate a personal and transformative experience. It is an opportunity for you to intentionally set aside time each day to nourish your mind, body, and spirit and to invite God to work in and through you for your holistic well-being.

As you embark on this journey, may you experience a deeper connection with God, a greater awareness of yourself, and a renewed sense of purpose. May you be inspired to make positive changes in your life, embrace self-care, and align your thoughts, actions, and spirit with God's will. May this devotional be a source of encouragement, guidance, and transformation as you nurture your mind, body, and spirit.

May this 365-day journey be a stepping stone toward a more fulfilling and abundant life where you experience the fullness of God's love, bliss, and peace. May you be transformed from the inside out, and may the fruits of this transformation overflow into every area of your life.

Encouragement to embark on a transformative journey of self-discovery and growth

Embarking on a transformative journey of self-discovery and growth is a courageous and rewarding decision. It requires a willingness to explore new depths within yourself, confront limiting beliefs, and embrace the possibilities of personal transformation. As you take this step, I want to offer you words of encouragement and support.

You are embarking on a path that has the potential to bring about profound changes in your life. This journey is an invitation to explore the vastness of who you are, to uncover hidden strengths, and to challenge the narratives that hold you back. It is an opportunity to step into your true identity, to align your life with your values, and to live authentically.

While this journey may have its moments of uncertainty and discomfort, remember that growth often happens outside of our comfort zones. Embrace the process of self-discovery with an open heart and mind. Be patient with yourself, for true transformation takes time. Allow yourself to make mistakes, learn from them, and keep moving forward.

As you delve into the depths of self-exploration, be kind and compassionate to yourself. Celebrate your progress, no matter how small, and extend grace to yourself in moments of setbacks. Remember that this journey is not about achieving perfection but rather about embracing growth and self-acceptance.

Surround yourself with a supportive community of like-minded individuals who can offer guidance, encouragement, and accountability. Seek out mentors, counselors, or spiritual leaders who can provide valuable insights and perspectives along your path. Share your journey with trusted friends or loved ones who can walk alongside you and provide support.

Above all, remember that you are not alone on this journey. As you embark on this transformative path, invite God to be your guide and companion. Lean on His wisdom, strength, and grace. Seek His guidance through prayer, meditation, and reflection. Allow Him to reveal the depths of your true self and guide you toward a life that is aligned with His purpose for you.

So, my friend, embrace this transformative journey with anticipation, determination and hope. Believe in the limitless potential within you and trust that as you invest in your personal growth, you will experience the beauty of becoming the best version of yourself. May this journey be filled with self-discovery, growth, and a deep sense of fulfillment. You are capable, you are deserving, and you are ready. Embrace the transformation that awaits you with open arms.

WELCOME TO THE MONTH OF JANUARY –
THEME: SELF-DISCOVERY AND AWARENESS

JANUARY 1

The Journey Begins: Embracing Self-Discovery

Bible Verse:

"Keep vigilant watch over your heart; that's where life starts." — Proverbs 4:23 (MSG)

Commentary:

The beginning of a journey is often filled with excitement and anticipation. As we embark on this path of self-discovery, it's essential to keep a watchful eye on our hearts. Proverbs remind us that our innermost thoughts and feelings are the wellspring of life, nurturing our spirit and fueling our journey. To truly transform, we must first understand what resides within us. Self-discovery is not just about finding who we are but also about cultivating a heart that reflects the values and virtues we hold dear. When we commit to knowing ourselves deeply, we lay a solid foundation for a life that is aligned with God's purpose.

Prayer:

Heavenly Father, thank You for the gift of a new journey. Help me to keep my heart open and vigilant as I embark on this path of self-discovery. Guide me to understand myself better and align my life with Your purpose. May my journey lead to transformation that glorifies You. In Jesus' name, Amen.

JANUARY 2

Who Am I? Exploring Your Identity

Bible Verse:

"So, God created human beings; He created them godlike, reflecting God's nature." — Genesis 1:27 (MSG)

Commentary:

Our identity is deeply rooted in the truth that we are created in the image of God. When we ask, "Who am I?" we are reminded that we are a reflection of God's nature. This means that we have inherent value, purpose, and dignity. Exploring our identity isn't just about our traits, likes, or dislikes; it's about understanding how we are uniquely fashioned to reflect God's might and glory. As we dig deeper into who we are, we must remember that our true identity is anchored in God's design and His divine purpose for our lives.

Prayer:

Lord, thank You for creating me in Your image. Help me to see myself through Your eyes and to recognize the unique qualities You have given me. Guide me as I explore my identity so that I may reflect Your nature in all I do. Amen.

JANUARY 3

Values and Beliefs: What Do I Stand For?

Bible Verse:

"For where your treasure is, there your heart will be also." — Matthew 6:21 (MSG)

Commentary:

Our values and beliefs are like treasures that we hold close to our hearts. They guide our decisions, shape our actions, and define what we stand for. Jesus teaches that what we treasure reveals the true condition of our hearts. To understand what we stand for, we must examine where our time, energy, and resources are invested. Are they aligned with God's Word and His desires for us? As we identify our core values and beliefs, let's make sure they reflect the principles of love, integrity, and faithfulness that Jesus taught.

Prayer:

Father God, help me to examine my heart and uncover the values and beliefs that guide my life. May my treasures be aligned with Your will, and may my heart be steadfast in living out the truths of Your Word. Teach me to stand firm in my convictions and to glorify You in all I do. In Jesus' name, Amen.

JANUARY 4

Uncovering Your Strengths and Weaknesses

Bible Verse:

"Each of us is an original. We must not be in a false image of ourselves." — Romans 12:3 (MSG)

Commentary:

Understanding our strengths and weaknesses is an essential part of self-discovery. God has created each of us uniquely, with different gifts and abilities. It's important to recognize and celebrate the strengths He has given us while also being aware of our weaknesses. This awareness of ourselves helps us grow and depend on God for the areas where we need improvement. When we acknowledge both our strengths and weaknesses, we can serve God more effectively and authentically.

Prayer:

Dear Lord, thank You for the unique strengths and gifts You have placed within me. Help me to use them for Your glory. Please give me the humility to recognize my weaknesses and the courage to work on them. Teach me to rely on Your strength in all things. Amen.

JANUARY 5

The Power of Self-Reflection

Bible Verse:

"Search me, God, and know my heart; test me and know my anxious thoughts." — Psalm 139:23 (MSG)

Commentary:

Self-reflection is a powerful tool for personal growth and transformation. By inviting God to search our hearts, we open ourselves to His divine insight and correction. This process of introspection helps us become more aware of our thoughts, actions, and intentions. It's through honest reflection that we can identify areas of our lives that need change and seek God's guidance for growth. Remember, self-reflection and introspection isn't about dwelling on our shortcomings but about recognizing where God's grace can bring transformation.

Prayer:

Lord, I invite You to search my heart and reveal any areas that need Your touch. Help me to reflect honestly on my life and make the necessary changes to grow closer to You. Guide me in this journey of self-discovery, and let Your Spirit lead me into all truth. In Jesus' name, Amen.

JANUARY 6

Recognizing Your Passions and Interests

Bible Verse:

"And don't be wishing you were someplace else or with someone else. Where you are right now is God's place for you." — 1 Corinthians 7:17 (MSG)

Commentary:

God has placed within each of us distinct passions and interests that align with His purpose for our lives. Recognizing what excites and inspires us is an essential step in self-discovery. Often, our passions are God's way of pointing us toward our calling. By embracing where we are and what we love, we can start to see God's hand in our lives more clearly. Reflecting on our passions helps us understand how God wants to use our unique gifts and interests to serve Him and others.

Prayer:

Heavenly Father, thank You for the passions and interests You have placed within me. Help me to recognize them as gifts from You and guide me to use them for Your glory. Teach me to be content with where I am and to trust that You have a purpose for my passions. May I always seek to align my desires with Your will. In Jesus' name, Amen.

JANUARY 7

Understanding Your Personality

Bible Verse:

"Before I shaped you in the womb, I knew all about you. Before you saw the light of DAY, I had holy plans for you." — Jeremiah 1:5 (MSG)

Commentary:

Our personalities are a part of the unique design God has for each of us. Understanding our personality traits can help us gain insight into how we relate to others and navigate the world. God knew us before we were born and intricately crafted every aspect of who we are, including our unique personalities. Whether we are introverted or extroverted, analytical or creative, God has a purpose for our particular traits. Embracing our personalities and understanding how they fit into God's plan can help us live more authentically and fulfill our divine purpose.

Prayer:

Dear Lord, thank You for the unique personality You have given me. Help me to understand myself better and use my traits to serve Your purpose. Guide me to accept and appreciate who I am, knowing that You created me with a specific plan in mind. May my life reflect Your love and wisdom in all my interactions. In Jesus' name, Amen.

JANUARY 8

Mindful Awareness: Observing Your Thoughts

Bible Verse:

"Fix your thoughts on what is true, and honorable, and right, and pure, and lovely, and admirable. Think about things that are excellent and worthy of praise."
— Philippians 4:8 (MSG)

Commentary:

Our thoughts shape our reality and influence our actions. Mindful awareness involves observing our thoughts without judgment and understanding their impact on our lives. The Bible encourages us to focus on thoughts that are true, honorable, and pure. By being mindful of our thought patterns, we can align them with God's truth and His desires for us. Observing our thoughts helps us to identify negative patterns and replace them with positive, life-affirming beliefs that lead to inner transformation.

Prayer:

Lord, help me to be mindful of my thoughts today. Teach me to observe them without judgment and to focus on what is true and good. Guide me to align my thinking with Your Word and let my mind be filled with thoughts that honor You. In Jesus' name, Amen.

JANUARY 9

Emotional Awareness: Understanding Your Feelings

Bible Verse:

"But the fruit of the Spirit is love, joy, peace, forbearance, kindness, goodness, faithfulness, gentleness, and self-control." — Galatians 5:22-23 (MSG)

Commentary:

Emotional awareness is about recognizing and understanding our feelings. Emotions are a natural part of being human, but how well we manage them is key to our spiritual growth. The Bible speaks of the fruits of the Spirit, which include qualities that reflect God's character. By becoming more aware of our emotions and learning to manage them through the Holy Spirit's guidance, we can cultivate these fruits in our lives. Understanding our feelings helps us respond to situations with love, patience, and self-control, reflecting God's nature in our actions.

Prayer:

Heavenly Father, thank You for the emotions You have given me. Help me to understand my feelings and manage them in a way that reflects Your Spirit. Guide me to cultivate love, joy, peace, and all the fruits of the Spirit in my life. May I respond to every situation with grace and wisdom. In Jesus' name, Amen.

JANUARY 10

Identifying Your Triggers

Bible Verse:

"A gentle answer deflects anger, but harsh words make tempers flare." — Proverbs 15:1 (MSG)

Commentary:

Triggers are emotional responses to certain situations or words that can lead to negative reactions. Identifying what triggers us is an important step in becoming more self-aware. When we recognize our triggers, we can prepare ourselves to respond calmly and thoughtfully instead of reacting impulsively. The Bible encourages us to respond with gentle answers that deflect anger and promote peace. By understanding our triggers, we can learn to manage our reactions and choose responses that align with God's love and wisdom.

Prayer:

Lord, help me recognize my triggers and understand the reasons behind them. Give me the wisdom to respond with calmness and grace, reflecting Your love in all my interactions. Teach me to manage my reactions and to choose words that build others up and bring peace. In Jesus' name, Amen.

JANUARY 11

Self-Awareness in Relationships

Bible Verse:

"Do to others as you would have them do to you." — Luke 6:31 (MSG)

Commentary:

Self-awareness plays a crucial role in our relationships. Understanding our thoughts, emotions, and behaviors helps us interact with others in a more compassionate and empathetic way. The Bible teaches us to treat others as we would like to be treated, a principle that requires a deep understanding of ourselves and our actions. By being mindful of how our words and actions affect others, we can cultivate stronger, healthier relationships that reflect God's love.

Prayer:

Father, thank You for the relationships You have blessed me with. Help me to be self-aware in my interactions, understanding how my words and actions impact others. Teach me to treat others with love, kindness, and respect, reflecting Your character in all my relationships. In Jesus' name, Amen.

JANUARY 12

Listening to Your Inner Voice

Bible Verse:

"Whether you turn to the right or to the left, your ears will hear a voice behind you, saying, 'This is the way; walk in it.'" — Isaiah 30:21 (MSG)

Commentary:

Our inner voice, or conscience, is a guide that helps us navigate life's choices. God often speaks to us through this inner voice, providing direction and wisdom. Listening to this voice requires stillness and attentiveness, qualities that are cultivated through prayer and meditation. By tuning in to our inner voice, we can discern God's will for our lives and make decisions that are aligned with His purpose. Trusting this divine guidance empowers us to walk on the path that God has set before us.

Prayer:

Lord, help me to listen to my inner voice, the whisper of Your guidance. Teach me to discern Your will for my life and to trust Your direction. May I always be attentive to Your voice and obedient to Your leading. In Jesus' name, Amen.

JANUARY 13

Patterns of Behavior: What Drives You?

Bible Verse:

"Search me, God, and know my heart; test me and know my anxious thoughts."— Psalm 139:23 (MSG)

Commentary:

Our behaviors often reveal patterns that are driven by underlying thoughts and beliefs. Understanding what drives our actions helps us identify areas that need change and growth. The psalmist invites God to search his heart and reveal his inner thoughts, a practice that leads to greater self-awareness and transformation. By examining our behaviors and asking God to reveal the motivations behind them, we can align our actions with His will and embark on a path of righteousness.

Prayer:

Heavenly Father, search my heart and reveal the patterns that drive my behavior. Help me to understand my motivations and align them with Your will. Teach me to act in ways that honor You and reflect Your love. Please guide me in the path of righteousness. In Jesus' name, Amen.

JANUARY 14

Exploring Your Inner Dialogue

Bible Verse:

"May these words of my mouth and this meditation of my heart be pleasing in your sight, Lord, my Rock and my Redeemer." — Psalm 19:14 (MSG)

Commentary:

Our inner dialogue, the way we talk to ourselves, significantly influences our self-perception and shapes our actions. Positive self-talk can encourage and uplift us, while negative self-talk can hinder our growth and spiritual journey. The Bible encourages us to meditate on words and thoughts that are pleasing to God, aligning our inner dialogue with His truth. By becoming aware of our self-talk and choosing words that reflect God's love and truth, we can foster a positive, faith-filled mindset that supports our inner transformation.

Prayer:

Lord, help me to be mindful of my inner dialogue and to choose words that are pleasing to You. Teach me to speak to myself with kindness, love, and truth, reflecting Your Word in my thoughts. May my inner dialogue uplift and encourage me in my journey of faith. In Jesus' name, Amen.

JANUARY 15

The Importance of Authenticity

Bible Verse:

"But God, who knows the heart, showed that he accepted them by giving the Holy Spirit to them, just as he did to us."— Acts 15:8 (MSG)

Commentary:

Authenticity is about being true to who we are without pretense or falsehood. God knows our hearts and sees us as we truly are, beyond any masks we may wear. Living authentically means embracing our true selves, as God created us, and being honest with ourselves and others. When we are authentic, we allow God's Spirit to work through us more effectively. Embracing authenticity opens the door to sincere relationships and spiritual growth, helping us live in a way that honors God.

Prayer:

Heavenly Father, thank You for knowing my heart and accepting me as I am. Help me to live authentically, embracing the person You created me to be. Teach me to be honest with myself and others, allowing Your Spirit to work through me. May my life reflect Your truth and love in all I do. In Jesus' name, Amen.

JANUARY 16

Shedding Social Masks

Bible Verse:

"Let us not become weary in doing good, for at the proper time we will reap a harvest if we do not give up." — Galatians 6:9 (MSG)

Commentary:

We often wear social masks to fit in or gain acceptance from others, but these masks can prevent us from living authentically. Shedding these masks requires courage and perseverance, as it means being vulnerable and showing our true selves. The Bible encourages us not to grow weary in doing good, even when it's challenging. By releasing the need to please others and focusing on pleasing God, we can live more freely and authentically, reaping the harvest of peace and joy that comes from being true to ourselves.

Prayer:

Lord, help me to shed the social masks I wear and embrace my true self. Give me the courage to be vulnerable and authentic, trusting that You accept me just as I am. Teach me to focus on pleasing You rather than seeking the approval of others. May I live in a way that reflects Your love and truth. In Jesus' name, Amen.

JANUARY 17

Living in Alignment with Your True Self

Bible Verse:

"Do not conform to the pattern of this world, but be transformed by the renewing of your mind." — Romans 12:2 (MSG)

Commentary:

Living in alignment with our true selves means not conforming to the expectations or patterns of the world but instead being transformed by God's truth. When we renew our minds with God's Word, we begin to see ourselves as He sees us, free from the pressures to be something we're not. Authenticity involves aligning our actions, thoughts, and beliefs with our true identity in Christ. By embracing who God created us to be, we can live a life that is genuine and fulfilling, reflecting His glory in all we do.

Prayer:

Father, help me to live in alignment with my true self, as You created me to be. Teach me not to conform to the world's expectations but to be transformed by Your truth. Renew my mind with Your Word, and guide me to live authentically in a way that honors You. In Jesus' name, Amen.

JANUARY 18

Facing Your Fears: What Holds You Back?

Bible Verse:

"So do not fear, for I am with you; do not be dismayed, for I am your God." — Isaiah 41:10 (MSG)

Commentary:

Fear can often hold us back from being our authentic selves. It might be the fear of rejection, failure, or judgment. But God reassures us that He is always with us, and we need not be afraid. Facing our fears requires us to trust and have faith in God's presence and His promises. When we confront what holds us back, we can move forward with confidence, knowing that God is by our side. Overcoming fear is a vital step in embracing authenticity and living fully in God's purpose.

Prayer:

Lord, help me to face my fears and recognize what holds me back from being my authentic self. Give me the courage to confront these fears, trusting that You are with me. Remind me of Your promise to never leave me or forsake me, and guide me to live boldly and authentically for You. In Jesus' name, Amen.

JANUARY 19

Accepting Your Imperfections

Bible Verse:

"But he said to me, 'My grace is sufficient for you, for my power is made perfect in weakness.'" — 2 Corinthians 12:9 (MSG)

Commentary:

We all have imperfections, but it's important to remember that God's grace is sufficient for us. Accepting our imperfections means acknowledging our humanity and recognizing that we are not perfect. It's through our weaknesses that God's power is made perfect. Embracing our flaws and limitations allows us to rely on God's strength and grace. When we accept ourselves as we are, without striving for perfection, we can live more authentically, confident in knowing that we are loved and valued by God just as we are.

Prayer:

Heavenly Father, thank You for Your grace that is sufficient for me. Help me to accept my imperfections and recognize that Your power is made perfect in my weakness. Teach me to rely on Your strength and grace in all things and to live authentically as the person You created me to be. In Jesu' name, Amen.

JANUARY 20

The Role of Vulnerability in Authenticity

Bible Verse:

"But if we walk in the light, as he is in the light, we have fellowship with one another." — 1 John 1:7 (MSG)

Commentary:

Vulnerability is a key component of authenticity. It involves being open and honest about our struggles, fears, and imperfections. Walking in the light, as God is in the light, means being transparent and genuine in our relationships with others. When we allow ourselves to be vulnerable, we create deeper connections and foster true fellowship. Vulnerability requires courage, but it brings freedom and healing. By embracing vulnerability, we can live more authentically and experience the fullness of God's love and grace in our lives.

Prayer:

Lord, give me the courage to be vulnerable and open with others. Help me to walk in the light, as You are in the light, and to build genuine relationships based on honesty and trust. Teach me to embrace vulnerability as a pathway to authenticity and a deeper connection with You and others. In Jesus' name, Amen.

JANUARY 21

Celebrating Your Uniqueness

Bible Verse:

"For we are God's masterpiece. He has created us anew in Christ Jesus, so we can do the good things he planned for us long ago." — Ephesians 2:10 (MSG)

Commentary:

God uniquely created each of us with a specific purpose and design. Celebrating our uniqueness means recognizing that we are God's masterpiece, created to fulfill a special role in His plan. When we embrace our individuality and the gifts and talents God has given us, we can live authentically and confidently. Celebrating who we are helps us to appreciate the diversity of God's creation and to see the beauty in being different. By acknowledging and celebrating our uniqueness, we honor God's creativity and His plan for our lives.

Prayer:

Heavenly Father, thank You for creating me as Your unique masterpiece. Help me to celebrate my individuality and the gifts You have given me. Teach me to embrace my uniqueness and to use it for Your glory. May I live authentically, honoring Your creativity and Your plan for my life. In Jesus' name, Amen.

JANUARY 22

Defining Your Purpose

Bible Verse:

"For I know the plans I have for you," declares the Lord, "plans to prosper you and not to harm you, plans to give you hope and a future." — Jeremiah 29:11 (MSG)

Commentary:

Understanding our purpose is a vital part of our spiritual voyage. God has a unique plan for each of our lives, filled with hope and a future. Defining your purpose involves seeking God's guidance and aligning your desires with His will. When we understand the purpose for which we were created, we can live intentionally and with direction. Knowing our purpose gives us a sense of meaning and fulfillment as we strive to glorify God in all we do.

Prayer:

Heavenly Father, thank You for the unique plan You have for my life. Help me to seek Your guidance and to understand my purpose according to Your will. May I live each DAY with intention, knowing that my life is in Your hands and that You have a hopeful future planned for me. In Jesus' name, Amen.

JANUARY 23

Setting Intentions for Personal Growth

Bible Verse:

"Commit to the Lord whatever you do, and he will establish your plans." — Proverbs 16:3 (MSG)

Commentary:

Setting intentions for personal growth is about committing our actions and goals to the Lord. When we align our intentions with God's will, He establishes our plans and directs our steps. Intentions focus on the purpose behind our actions, helping us to grow spiritually and personally. By being intentional in our pursuit of growth, we invite God's guidance and wisdom into our journey, ensuring that our efforts are fruitful and aligned with His purpose for our lives.

Prayer:

Lord, I commit my intentions for growth to You. Help me to align my actions with Your will and to seek Your guidance in all that I do. Establish my plans according to Your purpose, and guide me on the path of spiritual and personal growth. In Jesus' name, Amen.

JANUARY 24

Creating a Vision for Your Future

Bible Verse:

"Where there is no vision, the people perish; but blessed is the one who heeds wisdom's instruction."
— Proverbs 29:18 (MSG)

Commentary:

Having a clear vision for the future is essential for spiritual growth and contentment. A vision gives us direction and helps us focus on what truly matters. The Bible teaches that without a vision, people lose their way, but those who follow God's wisdom are blessed. Creating a vision for your future involves seeking God's guidance and harmonizing your dreams with His plans. When we have a vision, we can make choices that lead us toward God's purpose for our lives.

Prayer:

Heavenly Father, help me to create a vision for my future that aligns with Your plans. Guide me with Your wisdom and give me the clarity to see the path You have set before me. May I live each DAY with purpose and direction, following Your will for my life. In Jesus' name, Amen.

JANUARY 25

Identifying Limiting Beliefs

Bible Verse:

"For God has not given us a spirit of fear, but of power, love, and self-discipline." — 2 Timothy 1:7 (MSG)

Commentary:

Limiting beliefs are thoughts that hold us back from reaching our full potential in Christ. These beliefs often stem from fear, doubt, or past experiences. However, God has bestowed us a spirit of power, love, and self-discipline, not fear. Identifying and challenging our limiting beliefs is crucial for spiritual growth. By recognizing these negative thoughts and replacing them with God's truth, we can overcome obstacles and live boldly in the freedom and power of the Holy Spirit.

Prayer:

Lord, help me to identify and overcome any limiting beliefs that hold me back from fulfilling Your purpose. Replace my fear and doubt with Your truth, and fill me with a spirit of power, love, and self-discipline. Guide me to live boldly and confidently in Your promises. In Jesus' name, Amen.

JANUARY 26

Developing a Growth Mindset

Bible Verse:

"Consider it pure joy, my brothers and sisters, whenever you face trials of many kinds, because you know that the testing of your faith produces perseverance." — James 1:2-3 (MSG)

Commentary:

A growth mindset is the belief that challenges and setbacks are opportunities for growth and learning. The Bible encourages us to consider it pure joy when we face trials, knowing that these experiences develop perseverance and reinforce our faith. Developing a growth mindset involves trusting in God's purpose for our trials and believing that He is working all things for our good. By embracing a growth mindset, we can face challenges with resilience and hope, knowing that they are shaping us into the people God created us to be.

Prayer:

Heavenly Father, help me to develop a growth mindset and to see challenges as opportunities for growth. Strengthen my faith and give me the perseverance to overcome trials with joy and confidence in Your plan. May I trust in Your purpose for my life and embrace every experience as a chance to grow closer to You. In Jesus' name, Amen.

JANUARY 27

Setting Personal Boundaries

Bible Verse:

"Above all else, guard your heart, for everything you do flows from it." — Proverbs 4:23 (MSG)

Commentary:

Personal boundaries are essential for maintaining spiritual health and well-being. The Bible teaches us to guard our hearts, for everything we do flows from them. Setting boundaries helps us protect our hearts from harmful influences and maintain focus on God's will. By establishing what is acceptable in our relationships and daily lives, we create space for God's peace and guidance. Boundaries are not about isolation; they are about creating a healthy environment for spiritual growth and authentic living.

Prayer:

Lord, help me to set healthy boundaries that protect my heart and align with Your will. Teach me to guard my heart and to create space for Your peace and guidance. Give me the wisdom to know what is acceptable and the courage to enforce these boundaries in my life. In Jesus' name, Amen.

JANUARY 28

Self-Compassion: Being Kind to Yourself

Bible Verse:

"The Lord is gracious and compassionate, slow to anger and rich in love." — Psalm 145:8 (MSG)

Commentary:

Self-compassion involves treating ourselves with the same kindness and understanding that we would offer to others. God is gracious and compassionate, and He calls us to extend that same grace to ourselves. Being kind to ourselves means recognizing our humanity and extending forgiveness to ourselves for our mistakes. It's about embracing God's love and allowing His grace to cover our shortcomings. By practicing self-compassion, we can grow in self-awareness and spiritual maturity, knowing that we are loved and valued by God just as we are.

Prayer:

Heavenly Father, thank You for Your grace and compassion toward me. Help me to be kind to myself and to extend the same love and understanding that You have shown me. Teach me to forgive myself for my mistakes and to embrace Your grace in all areas of my life. May I grow in self-awareness and spiritual maturity, reflecting Your love in all I do. In Jesus' name, Amen.

JANUARY 29

Journaling for Self-Discovery

Bible Verse:

"Write down the revelation and make it plain on tablets so that a herald may run with it." — Habakkuk 2:2 (MSG)

Commentary:

Journaling is a powerful tool for self-discovery and spiritual growth. Writing down our thoughts, prayers, and reflections allows us to see God's work in our lives more clearly. The Bible encourages us to write down revelations and make them plain, helping us remember and act on God's guidance. Journaling helps us process our experiences, understand and regulate our emotions, and deepen our relationship with God. By taking time to write, we create space for reflection and growth, allowing God's truth to shape our hearts and minds.

Prayer:

Lord, help me to use journaling as a tool for self-discovery and spiritual growth. Guide my thoughts and reflections, and reveal Your truth to me as I write. May my journaling deepen my relationship with You and help me to see Your work in my life more clearly. In Jesus' name, Amen.

JANUARY 30

Reflecting on Your Journey So Far

Bible Verse:

"Remember the former things, those of long ago; I am God, and there is no other; I am God, and there is none like me." — Isaiah 46:9 (MSG)

Commentary:

Reflecting on our journey allows us to see how far we've come and recognize God's presence in our lives. The Bible inspires us to remember the past and acknowledge God's faithfulness. Reflecting helps us appreciate our development and understand the lessons we've learned. It also allows us to see areas where we still need to grow and to seek God's guidance for the future. By taking time to reflect, we can celebrate our progress and renew our commitment to living according to God's purpose.

Prayer:

Heavenly Father, thank You for guiding me on this journey of self-discovery and growth. Help me to reflect on how far I've come and to recognize Your presence in my life. Teach me to appreciate my growth and to seek Your guidance for the areas where I still need to grow. May I continue to walk in Your purpose and trust in Your faithfulness. In Jesus' name, Amen.

JANUARY 31

Anticipating the Future

Bible Verse:

"For I know the plans I have for you," declares the Lord, "plans to prosper you and not to harm you, plans to give you hope and a future." — Jeremiah 29:11 (MSG)

Commentary:

Anticipating the future involves looking forward with hope and confidence in God's plans for your life. Jeremiah 29:11 reminds us that God has plans to prosper us and give us hope and a future. As you reflect on the past year and prepare for the coming one, have faith that God is working in every detail of your life. By placing your hope in His promises, you can face the future with optimism and assurance, knowing that He is guiding your path and has good things in store for you.

Prayer:

Heavenly Father, help me to anticipate the future with hope and confidence in Your plans. Teach me to trust in Your promises and to look forward with faith in Your guidance and love. Amen.

WELCOME TO THE MONTH OF FEBRUARY –
THEME: POSITIVE MINDSET

FEBRUARY 1

The Power of Positive Thinking

Bible Verse:

"Finally, brothers and sisters, whatever is true, whatever is noble, whatever is right, whatever is pure, whatever is lovely, whatever is admirable—if anything is excellent or praiseworthy—think about such things." — Philippians 4:8 (MSG)

Commentary:

Positive thinking is more than just an optimistic outlook; it's about aligning our thoughts with God's truth. Philippians 4:8 encourages us to focus on what is noble, right, pure, lovely, and admirable. When we deliberately choose to think positively, we allow God's peace and joy to fill our hearts and minds. This mindset enables us to see situations from God's perspective, lessens anxiety, and fosters hope. By practicing positive thinking, we can overcome negative patterns and develop a resilient, faith-filled attitude that honors God and blesses others.

Prayer:

Lord, help me focus my thoughts on what is good and true. Fill my mind with positivity that reflects Your love and peace. May my thoughts honor You today. Amen.

FEBRUARY 2

Choosing Joy in Every Situation

Bible Verse:

"Consider it pure joy, my brothers and sisters, whenever you face trials of many kinds." — James 1:2 (MSG)

Commentary:

Choosing joy doesn't mean turning a blind eye to life's difficulties; it means trusting God amidst them. James 1:2 reminds us that trials are opportunities for growth and spiritual maturity. Joy is a fruit of the Spirit that comes from our relationship with God, not our circumstances. When we choose joy, we affirm our faith in God's goodness and sovereignty, even when things are tough. This choice transforms our outlook and strengthens our spirit, allowing us to experience God's peace and purpose in every situation.

Prayer:

Heavenly Father, teach me to choose joy in every situation. Help me see trials as opportunities for growth and to trust in Your goodness. Fill my heart with the joy that comes from You. Amen.

FEBRUARY 3

Focusing on Gratitude

Bible Verse:

"Give thanks in all circumstances, for this is God's will for you in Christ Jesus." — 1 Thessalonians 5:18 (MSG)

Commentary:

Gratitude is a powerful tool for cultivating a positive mindset. 1 Thessalonians 5:18 tells us to give thanks in all circumstances, recognizing that gratitude aligns us with God's will. By focusing on what we are grateful for, we shift our perspective from what we lack to what we have, fostering contentment and bliss. Gratitude opens our hearts to God's presence and reminds us of His constant blessings. When we practice gratitude daily, we become more aware of God's goodness, which fuels a positive outlook on life.

Prayer:

Lord, help me to cultivate a heart of gratitude. Remind me to give thanks in all circumstances and to focus on Your blessings. May my gratitude draw me closer to You. Amen.

FEBRUARY 4

Speaking Life into Your Circumstances

Bible Verse:

"The tongue has the power of life and death, and those who love it will eat its fruit." — Proverbs 18:21 (MSG)

Commentary:

Our words have immense power to shape our reality and influence those around us. Proverbs 18:21 teaches that the tongue can bring life or death, depending on how we use it. Speaking life into our circumstances involves choosing words that build up, encourage, and reflect God's truth. When we speak positively, we align ourselves with God's promises and create an atmosphere of faith and hope. Our words can inspire and uplift not only ourselves but also others, transforming our environment and nurturing a positive mindset.

Prayer:

Heavenly Father, help me to speak words that bring life and reflect Your truth. Guide my tongue to encourage and build up others. May my words honor You and inspire hope. Amen.

FEBRUARY 5

Surrounding Yourself with Positivity

Bible Verse:

"Walk with the wise and become wise, for a companion of fools suffers harm." — Proverbs 13:20 (MSG)

Commentary:

The company we keep influences our mindset and attitudes significantly. Proverbs 13:20 reminds us that walking with the wise leads to wisdom, while negative influences can bring harm. Surrounding ourselves with positive, faith-filled people encourages growth and helps us maintain a hopeful perspective. By choosing friends and environments that uplift, augment and challenge us in our faith, we cultivate a mindset that reflects God's love and wisdom. Positive surroundings reinforce our spiritual journey and inspire us to live joyfully and purposefully.

Prayer:

Lord, guide me to surround myself with people and environments that encourage positivity and growth. Help me choose wisely and seek relationships that honor You. Amen.

FEBRUARY 6

Renewing Your Mind with God's Word

Bible Verse:

"Do not conform to the pattern of this world, but be transformed by the renewing of your mind." — Romans 12:2 (MSG)

Commentary:

Renewing our minds is a daily process that involves immersing ourselves in God's Word. Romans 12:2 urges us to transform by renewing our minds, which means replacing worldly thoughts with God's truth. Scripture shapes our thinking and aligns us with God's will, helping us cultivate a positive, devout mentality. By meditating on God's Word, we are reminded of His promises and encouraged to trust in His plans. This renewal brings clarity, peace, and a deeper understanding of God's purpose for our lives.

Prayer:

Heavenly Father, help me to renew my mind with Your Word. Guide me to meditate on Your truth and transform my thoughts to align with Your will. Amen.

FEBRUARY 7

Overcoming Negative Self-Talk

Bible Verse:

"For as he thinks in his heart, so is he." — Proverbs 23:7 (MSG)

Commentary:

Negative self-talk can be a significant obstacle to cultivating a positive mindset. Proverbs 23:7 emphasizes that our thoughts shape who we are and how we live. Overcoming negative self-talk involves recognizing our detrimental thoughts and replacing them with God's truth. By affirming our identity in Christ and focusing on God's promises, we can shift our mindset from negativity to positivity. This practice helps us build confidence, self-worth, and resilience, enabling us to live as God intended—joyful, hopeful, and fully assured of His love.

Prayer:

Lord, help me to recognize and overcome negative self-talk. Fill my mind with Your truth and remind me of my worth in You. May my thoughts reflect Your love and grace. Amen.

FEBRUARY 8

Practicing Mindfulness

Bible Verse:

"Be still, and know that I am God." — Psalm 46:10 (MSG)

Commentary:

Mindfulness involves the practice of being present and fully engaged at the moment, aware of where we are and what we're doing. Psalm 46:10 encourages us to be still and recognize God's presence in our lives. Practicing mindfulness helps us slow down, notice God's blessings, and appreciate the beauty of each moment. It allows us to become more aware of our thoughts and feelings, creating space for God's peace and guidance. By cultivating mindfulness, we can develop a positive mindset that is rooted in the awareness of God's constant presence and love.

Prayer:

Lord, help me to practice mindfulness today. Teach me to be still and recognize Your presence in every moment. May I find peace and joy in being fully present with You. Amen.

FEBRUARY 9

Affirming Your Worth in Christ

Bible Verse:

"For we are God's masterpiece. He has created us anew in Christ Jesus, so we can do the good things he planned for us long ago." — Ephesians 2:10 (MSG)

Commentary:

Affirming your worth in Christ means recognizing that you are a unique and valuable creation of God. Ephesians 2:10 tells us that we are God's masterpiece, created anew in Christ Jesus. When we affirm our worth, we reject lies of inadequacy and embrace the truth of our identity in Christ. This positive habit fosters us in building confidence and self-esteem grounded in God's love. By regularly affirming who we are in Christ, we develop a mindset that is resilient, hopeful, and aligned with God's purpose for our lives.

Prayer:

Heavenly Father, thank You for creating me as Your masterpiece. Help me to affirm my worth in Christ and to live confidently in Your love and purpose. Amen.

FEBRUARY 10

Setting Daily Intentions

Bible Verse:

"Commit to the Lord whatever you do, and he will establish your plans." — Proverbs 16:3 (MSG)

Commentary:

Setting daily intentions involves beginning each DAY with a clear purpose aligned with God's will. Proverbs 16:3 encourages us to commit our actions to the Lord, trusting that He will guide our plans. By establishing positive intentions, we focus our thoughts and actions on what truly matters, allowing God to direct our path. This practice helps us stay mindful of our spiritual goals and remain focused throughout the DAY. By earnestly committing our intentions to God, we invite His guidance and support, creating a foundation for a positive, purpose-driven life.

Prayer:

Lord, I commit my intentions to You today. Guide my thoughts and actions according to Your will, and help me to stay focused on what matters most. Amen.

FEBRUARY 11

The Habit of Encouragement

Bible Verse:

"Therefore encourage one another and build each other up, just as in fact you are doing." — 1 Thessalonians 5:11 (MSG)

Commentary:

Encouragement is a powerful habit that fosters positivity and strengthens relationships. 1 Thessalonians 5:11 urges us to encourage one another and build each other up. When we make a habit of speaking words of affirmation, we uplift those around us and create a supportive, positive environment. Encouragement not only benefits others but also enriches our own lives by reinforcing a mindset of love and kindness. By focusing on the good in others and sharing words of encouragement and postitivity, we cultivate a spirit of positivity and reflect God's love.

Prayer:

Heavenly Father, help me to be an encourager today. Teach me to speak words that build others up and create a positive environment. May my words reflect Your love and kindness. Amen.

FEBRUARY 12

Celebrating Small Victories

Bible Verse:

"Do not despise these small beginnings, for the Lord rejoices to see the work begin." — Zechariah 4:10 (MSG)

Commentary:

Celebrating small victories is a practice that boosts progress and fosters a positive mindset. Zechariah 4:10 reminds us not to despise small beginnings, for God rejoices in every step of growth. Acknowledging and celebrating little achievements helps us stay motivated and focused on our journey. Rejoicing celebrations remind us of God's faithfulness and encourage us to keep moving forward. By appreciating even the smallest victories, we develop a habit of gratitude and joy, recognizing that every step, no matter how small, is significant in our spiritual growth.

Prayer:

Lord, thank You for the progress I make each DAY. Help me to celebrate small victories and recognize Your work in my life. May I always be grateful for every step forward. Amen.

FEBRUARY 13

Letting Go of Comparison

Bible Verse:

"Pay careful attention to your own work, for then you will get the satisfaction of a job well done, and you won't need to compare yourself to anyone else."
— Galatians 6:4 (MSG)

Commentary:

Comparison can rob us of joy and hinder our spiritual growth. Galatians 6:4 encourages us to focus on our own work and find satisfaction in what we do rather than comparing ourselves to others. Letting go of our habit of comparison allows us to appreciate our unique journey and celebrate our own progress. By focusing on our strengths and what God has called us to do, we cultivate a positive mindset that is free from envy and competition. Embracing our individuality helps us live authentically and blissfully, trusting in God's plan for our lives.

Prayer:

Heavenly Father, help me to let go of comparison and focus on my unique journey. Teach me to appreciate my progress and trust in Your plan for my life. Amen.

Embracing Change with Positivity

Bible Verse:

"For I am about to do something new. See, I have already begun! Do you not see it?" — Isaiah 43:19 (MSG)

Commentary:

Change is an integral and constant part of life, and embracing it with optimism can lead to growth and transformation. Isaiah 43:19 reminds us that God is always at work, doing something new in our lives. When we embrace and view change with a positive attitude, we open ourselves to new opportunities and experiences that God has prepared for us. By trusting in God's plan and seeing change as a chance to grow, we cultivate resilience and adaptability. Embracing change with positivity allows us to move forward with confidence, knowing that God is guiding us every step of the way.

Prayer:

Lord, help me to embrace change with positivity and trust in Your plan for my life. Teach me to see new opportunities as a chance to grow and to move forward with confidence. Amen.

FEBRUARY 15

Identifying Your Triggers

Bible Verse:

"A person's wisdom yields patience; it is to one's glory to overlook an offense." — Proverbs 19:11 (MSG)

Commentary:

Identifying your triggers is crucial for maintaining a positive mindset. Proverbs 19:11 teaches us that wisdom leads to patience and that it's to our benefit to overlook offenses. By recognizing the situations, words, or behaviors that trigger negative emotions, we can prepare ourselves to respond with grace and patience. Understanding our triggers helps us to manage our reactions and choose responses that align with God's love and wisdom. This awareness empowers us to maintain peace and reinforce positivity within us, even when faced with challenging circumstances.

Prayer:

Lord, help me to identify and understand my triggers. Teach me to respond with patience and grace, reflecting Your wisdom and love in all my actions. Amen.

FEBRUARY 16

Practicing Forgiveness

Bible Verse:

"Be kind and compassionate to one another, forgiving each other, just as in Christ God forgave you." — Ephesians 4:32 (MSG)

Commentary:

Forgiveness is a powerful tool for cultivating a positive mindset. Ephesians 4:32 encourages us to be kind, compassionate, and forbearing, just as God has forgiven us through Christ. Holding onto grudges and bitterness can weigh us down and hinder our spiritual growth. By practicing forgiveness and forbearance, we release the negative emotions that hold us back and open our hearts to God's healing and peace. Forgiveness is not just about letting go of the past; it's about freeing ourselves to live happily and positively in the present.

Prayer:

Heavenly Father, help me to practice forgiveness and let go of any bitterness or resentment. Fill my heart with Your compassion and kindness, and guide me to live with a forgiving spirit. Amen.

FEBRUARY 17

Releasing the Need for Control

Bible Verse:

"Trust in the Lord with all your heart and lean not on your own understanding." — Proverbs 3:5 (MSG)

Commentary:

Releasing the need for control is essential for a positive mindset. Proverbs 3:5 reminds us to trust in the Lord with all our hearts and not rely on our understanding. When we try to control every aspect of our lives, we often become anxious and frustrated. Trusting God means surrendering our desire for control and believing that His plans are always better than ours. By releasing control and trusting in God's wisdom, we find peace and true liberty. This act of surrender helps us focus on what truly matters and maintain a positive outlook, knowing that God is in charge.

Prayer:

Lord, help me to release my need for control and trust in Your perfect plan. Teach me to rely on Your wisdom and to find peace in surrendering to Your will. Amen.

FEBRUARY 18

Navigating Difficult Conversations Positively

Bible Verse:

"Let your conversation be always full of grace, seasoned with salt, so that you may know how to answer everyone." — Colossians 4:6 (MSG)

Commentary:

Difficult conversations can be challenging, but positively navigating them is key to maintaining healthy relationships. Colossians 4:6 encourages us to speak with grace and wisdom, allowing us to respond appropriately to others. When we approach difficult conversations with a positive attitude, we create an environment of understanding and respect. By listening carefully and speaking kindly, we reflect God's love and promote healing and reconciliation. Handling these conversations well not only strengthens our relationships but also helps us maintain a positive mindset in all interactions.

Prayer:

Heavenly Father, guide me in navigating difficult conversations with grace and wisdom. Help me to listen with empathy and speak with kindness, reflecting Your love in all I say and do. Amen.

FEBRUARY 19

Handling Criticism Constructively

Bible Verse:

"Whoever heeds life-giving correction will be at home among the wise." — Proverbs 15:31 (MSG)

Commentary:

Criticism, when handled constructively, can be an opportunity for growth. Proverbs 15:31 tells us that those who heed life-giving correction will be wise. Instead of reacting defensively to criticism, we can choose to see it as valuable feedback that helps us improve. By maintaining a positive attitude, we can discern constructive criticism from negativity and use it to grow stronger in our faith and character. Graciously accepting criticism shows humility and a willingness to learn, which fosters a positive mindset and deepens our spiritual maturity.

Prayer:

Lord, help me to handle criticism constructively and to see it as an opportunity for growth. Teach me to accept correction with humility and to learn from it, becoming wiser in Your truth. Amen.

FEBRUARY 20

Finding Peace in Uncertainty

Bible Verse:

"You will keep in perfect peace those whose minds are steadfast because they trust in you." — Isaiah 26:3 (MSG)

Commentary:

Uncertainty can often lead to agitation and fear, but finding peace in these moments is key to a positive mindset. Isaiah 26:3 promises perfect peace to those whose minds are steadfast and who trust in God. When we focus on God's unchanging character and trust in His promises, we can find peace even in uncertain times. Keeping our minds fixed on God helps us navigate the unknown with confidence, knowing that He is in control. Having unwavering faith in God's plan allows us to remain calm and positive despite the uncertainties we face.

Prayer:

Heavenly Father, help me to find peace in uncertainty by trusting in You. Keep my mind steadfast and focused on Your promises, and guide me to remain positive and hopeful in all circumstances. Amen.

Transforming Fear into Faith

Bible Verse:

"For God has not given us a spirit of fear, but of power and of love and of a sound mind." — 2 Timothy 1:7 (MSG)

Commentary:

Fear can be a significant hindrance to a positive mindset, but it can be transformed into faith through God's power. 2 Timothy 1:7 reminds us that God has not given us a spirit of fear but of power, love, and a sound mind. When fear threatens to overwhelm us, we can choose to focus on God's promises and trust in His strength. By replacing fear with faith, we affirm God's power and presence in our lives, enabling us to face challenges with reinforced courage and confidence. This transformation fosters a mindset of positivity, hope, and trust in God's goodness.

Prayer:

Lord, help me to transform my fear into faith by trusting in Your power and love. Guide me to focus on Your promises and to face challenges with courage and confidence. Amen.

FEBRUARY 22

Nurturing Hope

Bible Verse:

"May the God of hope fill you with all joy and peace as you trust in him, so that you may overflow with hope by the power of the Holy Spirit." — Romans 15:13 (MSG)

Commentary:

Hope is a powerful force that fuels a positive mindset. Romans 15:13 reminds us that God is the source of all hope and that trusting in Him fills us with joy and peace. Nurturing hope involves focusing on God's promises and trusting in His plan for our lives. By keeping our eyes on God's faithfulness, we can maintain a hopeful outlook, even in tough times. Hope anchors our souls and keeps us steady, reminding us that God is always working in our favor. It helps us see beyond our circumstances and believe in God's greater purpose.

Prayer:

Heavenly Father, fill me with Your hope today. Help me to trust in Your promises and to nurture a hopeful outlook. May Your joy and peace overflow in my heart. Amen.

FEBRUARY 23

Embracing Patience in the Process

Bible Verse:

"But if we hope for what we do not yet have, we wait for it patiently." — Romans 8:25 (MSG)

Commentary:

Patience is a vital component of cultivating a positive mindset. Romans 8:25 encourages us to wait patiently for what we hope for, trusting in God's perfect timing. Embracing patience means understanding that growth and change take time. It's about trusting that God is working in and through us, even when we don't see immediate results. Patience helps us to remain calm and positive, knowing that God's timing is always best. By practicing patience, we learn to appreciate the journey and trust that God is guiding us in all walks of life.

Prayer:

Lord, help me to embrace patience in the process. Teach me to trust in Your timing and to wait with a positive heart, knowing that You are at work in my life. Amen.

FEBRUARY 24

Maintaining Positivity in Stressful Situations

Bible Verse:

"Cast all your anxiety on him because he cares for you." — 1 Peter 5:7 (MSG)

Commentary:

Stressful situations can easily disrupt our peace and positivity, but we are encouraged to cast our anxieties in the hands of God. 1 Peter 5:7 reminds us that God cares for us and wants us to bring our worries to Him. By surrendering our stress to God, we invite His peace into our hearts and minds. Maintaining positivity in stressful times involves trusting that God is in complete control and believing that He will provide the strength and guidance we need. With God's help, we can remain calm and positive, even in the midst of challenges.

Prayer:

Heavenly Father, help me to cast my anxieties on You and trust in Your care. Teach me to maintain positivity in stressful situations, knowing that You are with me always. Amen.

FEBRUARY 25

Building Resilience Through Faith

Bible Verse:

"Consider it pure joy, my brothers and sisters, whenever you face trials of many kinds, because you know that the testing of your faith produces perseverance." — James 1:2-3 (MSG)

Commentary:

Resilience is the ability to bounce back from adversity, and it is attained and strengthened through faith. James 1:2-3 encourages us to consider trials as opportunities for growth, as they produce perseverance. Building resilience involves trusting in God's faithfulness and believing that He will see us through every challenge. When our faith is tested, we have the chance to grow stronger and more steadfast. By relying on God's strength and promises, we can develop a resilient, optimistic mindset that enables us to overcome difficulties and thrive.

Prayer:

Lord, help me to build resilience through faith. Teach me to trust in Your strength and to see challenges as opportunities for growth. May my faith grow stronger in every trial. Amen.

FEBRUARY 26

Fostering a Spirit of Generosity

Bible Verse:

"A generous person will prosper; whoever refreshes others will be refreshed." — Proverbs 11:25 (MSG)

Commentary:

Generosity is a powerful way to cultivate a progressive mindset. Proverbs 11:25 tells us that a generous person will prosper and that those who refresh others will themselves be refreshed. When we give freely of our time, resources, and love, we reflect God's heart and create an atmosphere of bliss and gratitude. Generosity shifts our focus from ourselves to others, fostering a sense of fulfillment and contentment. By fostering a spirit of generosity, we not only bless those around us but also experience the joy and refreshment that come from living a life of giving.

Prayer:

Heavenly Father, help me to foster a spirit of generosity. Teach me to give freely and joyfully, reflecting Your love to others. May my heart be filled with the joy of giving. Amen.

FEBRUARY 27

The Power of Worship in Shaping Mindset

Bible Verse:

"Come, let us bow down in worship, let us kneel before the Lord our Maker." — Psalm 95:6 (MSG)

Commentary:

Worship is a powerful weapon and act that shapes our mindset and aligns our hearts with God's truth. Psalm 95:6 invites us to bow down in worship, submission, and acknowledging God as our Creator and Lord. When we worship, we shift our focus from our circumstances to God's greatness and goodness. Worship fills our hearts with gratitude and reminds us of God's faithfulness. By making worship a regular part of our lives, we cultivate a mindset of praise and positivity, anchored in the knowledge of who God is and His love for us.

Prayer:

Lord, help me to worship You with all my heart. Teach me to focus on Your greatness and goodness, and let my worship shape my mindset and fill me with joy. Amen.

FEBRUARY 28

Visualizing God's Promises

Bible Verse:

"I meditate on your precepts and consider your ways." — Psalm 119:15 (MSG)

Commentary:

Visualizing God's promises helps us focus on His faithfulness and align our thoughts with His Word. Psalm 119:15 encourages us to meditate on God's precepts and consider His ways. By visualizing God's promises, we remind ourselves of His truth and keep our minds fixed on His goodness. This practice helps us develop a positive viewpoint grounded in the assurance of God's love and provision. When we visualize God's promises, we fortify our faith and cultivate a mindset of hope, trusting that God will fulfill His Word in our lives.

Prayer:

Heavenly Father, help me to visualize Your promises and meditate on Your Word. Strengthen my faith and fill my mind with the assurance of Your love and faithfulness. Amen.

WELCOME TO THE MONTH OF MARCH –
THEME: PHYSICAL WELLNESS AND SELF-CARE

MARCH 1

Understanding Your Body as a Temple

Bible Verse:

"Do you not know that your bodies are temples of the Holy Spirit, who is in you, whom you have received from God? You are not your own." — 1 Corinthians 6:19 (MSG)

Commentary:

The Bible teaches us that our bodies are temples of the Holy Spirit entrusted to us by God. Understanding our bodies as temples means recognizing the divine presence within us and honoring that with our actions. When we treat our bodies with respect, making choices that promote health and well-being, we glorify God. Taking care of our physical health is an act of worship, reflecting our gratitude for the life and the strength that God has given us. This perspective encourages us to make mindful decisions that support our overall wellness and spiritual growth.

Prayer:

Heavenly Father, thank You for the gift of my body. Help me to treat it as Your temple, making choices that honor You and promote health and wellness. Amen.

MARCH 2

The Importance of Nutrition

Bible Verse:

"So, whether you eat or drink or whatever you do, do it all for the glory of God."— 1 Corinthians 10:31 (MSG)

Commentary:

Nutrition plays a vital role in maintaining our physical and spiritual health. 1 Corinthians 10:31 reminds us to do everything, including eating and drinking, for the glory of God. Proper nutrition fuels our bodies and minds, enabling us to serve God more effectively. By choosing wholesome foods that nourish us, we honor God with our bodies and take a step toward holistic wellness. Focusing on nourishment helps us build a strong foundation for physical health, which is essential for sustaining our spiritual journey as well as living a life that glorifies God.

Prayer:

Lord, guide me to make nutritious choices that honor You. Help me to see food as a way to fuel my body and serve You better. Amen.

MARCH 3

Hydration: Water for the Body and Spirit

Bible Verse:

"But whoever drinks the water I give them will never thirst. Indeed, the water I give them will become in them a spring of water welling up to eternal life." — John 4:14 (MSG)

Commentary:

Water is essential for our physical health and well-being, just as spiritual hydration is vital for our soul. In John 4:14, Jesus speaks of living water that quenches our spiritual thirst. Just as our bodies need water to function properly, our spirits need the living water of Christ to thrive. Staying hydrated physically supports all bodily functions, while spiritual hydration nourishes our relationship with God. Both are essential for a balanced, healthy life. By prioritizing hydration, we care for our bodies and souls, recognizing God's provision in every drop.

Prayer:

Heavenly Father, thank You for the gift of water that nourishes my body. Help me also to drink deeply of Your living water, which sustains my spirit. Amen.

MARCH 4

The Benefits of Regular Exercise

Bible Verse:

"For physical training is of some value, but godliness has value for all things, holding promise for both the present life and the life to come." — 1 Timothy 4:8 (MSG)

Commentary:

Exercise is essential for maintaining physical health, but it also benefits our mental and spiritual well-being. 1 Timothy 4:8 acknowledges the value of physical training while emphasizing that godliness holds eternal value. Regular exercise helps enhance our strength, endurance, and overall health, enabling us to serve God more effectively. It also reduces stress and enhances mental clarity, fostering a positive mindset. By integrating exercise into our routine, we honor our bodies as God's creation and prepare ourselves to fulfill His purpose for our lives.

Prayer:

Lord, help me to value and incorporate regular exercise into my life. May my physical training strengthen me to serve You better and glorify You in all I do. Amen.

MARCH 5

Rest and Recovery: Honoring Sabbath Rest

Bible Verse:

"Then he said to them, 'The Sabbath was made for man, not man for the Sabbath.'" — Mark 2:27 (MSG)

Commentary:

Rest is a fundamental part of God's design for our lives. Mark 2:27 teaches us that the Sabbath was made for man, emphasizing the importance of rest and recovery. Just as our bodies need rest to heal and rejuvenate, our spirits need time to reconnect with God and reflect on His goodness. Honoring the Sabbath and prioritizing rest allows us to revitalize physically, mentally, and spiritually. By setting aside time for rest, we acknowledge our reliance on God and His provision, allowing Him to renew our strength and guide our steps.

Prayer:

Heavenly Father, teach me to honor the Sabbath and prioritize rest. Help me to find restoration in You and to trust in Your provision for my life. Amen.

MARCH 6

The Role of Sleep in Wellness

Bible Verse:

"In peace, I will lie down and sleep, for you alone, Lord, make me dwell in safety." — Psalm 4:8 (MSG)

Commentary:

Sleep is vital for our health and well-being. Psalm 4:8 reminds us that God provides safety and peace, allowing us to rest securely. Quality sleep is essential for physical recovery, mental clarity, and emotional balance. It also plays a crucial role in maintaining an equilibrium of positive mindset and spiritual focus. By prioritizing sleep, we care for the bodies God has given us and acknowledge our need for His peace and protection. Good sleep habits help us wake up refreshed, ready to face each DAY with energy and purpose.

Prayer:

Lord, thank You for the gift of sleep. Help me to rest in Your peace and trust in Your protection. May my sleep renew my body and spirit, preparing me for the DAYs ahead. Amen.

MARCH 7

Understanding Your Body's Signals

Bible Verse:

"I praise you because I am fearfully and wonderfully made; your works are wonderful; I know that full well." — Psalm 139:14 (MSG)

Commentary:

God created our bodies with remarkable complexity and wisdom. Psalm 139:14 acknowledges that we are fearfully and wonderfully made, highlighting the importance of understanding our bodies. Paying attention to our body's signals, such as hunger, fatigue, or discomfort, helps us care for our physical health effectively. Recognizing these signals allows us to respond appropriately, whether it's through nourishing food, rest, or medical attention. By listening to our bodies, we honor God's incredible creation and take proactive steps toward maintaining overall wellness and vitality.

Prayer:

Heavenly Father, thank You for creating me fearfully and wonderfully. Help me to listen to my body's signals and care for it as a gift from You. Guide me in making choices that honor You and promote health. Amen.

MARCH 8

Developing a Consistent Exercise Routine

Bible Verse:

"Do you not know that in a race, all the runners run, but only one gets the prize? Run in such a way as to get the prize." — 1 Corinthians 9:24 (MSG)

Commentary:

Developing a consistent exercise routine is key to maintaining physical health and honoring the body God has given us. 1 Corinthians 9:24 encourages us to run with purpose, suggesting the importance of discipline and commitment in our physical activities. Regular exercise strengthens our bodies, improves our mood, and enhances our energy levels, allowing us to serve God more effectively. By creating a consistent routine, we build endurance and cultivate discipline, both physically and spiritually, aligning our lives with God's desire for us to live healthily and purposefully.

Prayer:

Lord, help me to develop a consistent exercise routine that honors You. Lord, please give me the discipline and commitment to care for my body, running the race with purpose. Amen.

MARCH 9

Mindful Eating: Eating with Intention

Bible Verse:

"So, whether you eat or drink or whatever you do, do it all for the glory of God." — 1 Corinthians 10:31 (MSG)

Commentary:

Mindful eating is about being intentional with what and how we eat, recognizing food as a gift from God. 1 Corinthians 10:31 reminds us to do everything, including eating and drinking, for the glory of God. By eating mindfully, we become more aware of our food choices, savoring each bite with gratitude and avoiding overeating or consuming foods that do not nourish our bodies. This practice helps us develop a healthier relationship with food, honoring and recognizing God's provision and caring for the temple of the Holy Spirit within us.

Prayer:

Heavenly Father, guide me to eat mindfully and with gratitude. Help me to make choices that nourish my body and honor You in all I do. Amen.

MARCH 10

Establishing a Healthy Sleep Schedule

Bible Verse:

"When you lie down, you will not be afraid; when you lie down, your sleep will be sweet." — Proverbs 3:24 (MSG)

Commentary:

Establishing a healthy sleep schedule is essential for physical and mental well-being. Proverbs 3:24 assures us that when we trust in God, our sleep will be sweet and peaceful. A consistent sleep routine helps regulate our body's natural rhythms, promoting better rest and recovery. By prioritizing sleep, we allow our bodies to heal, recharge, and function optimally. A healthy sleep schedule not only benefits our physical health but also enhances our emotional and spiritual welfare, enabling us to start each DAY refreshed and ready to serve God.

Prayer:

Lord, help me establish a healthy sleep schedule that honors You. Grant me restful sleep, and renew my body and spirit for the DAY ahead. Amen.

MARCH 11

The Importance of Flexibility and Stretching

Bible Verse:

"She sets about her work vigorously; her arms are strong for her tasks." — Proverbs 31:17 (MSG)

Commentary:

Flexibility and stretching are crucial for maintaining physical health and preventing injuries. Proverbs 31:17 highlights the importance of being strong and prepared for our tasks. Incorporating stretching into our daily routine improves flexibility, reduces muscle tension, and enhances physical performance. Stretching also helps us become more aware of our bodies, promoting relaxation and mindfulness. By prioritizing flexibility, we care for our bodies and ensure that we are readily capable of fulfilling God's purposes for our lives with strength and vitality.

Prayer:

Heavenly Father, thank You for the gift of my body. Help me to prioritize flexibility and stretching, keeping my body strong and prepared for Your work. Amen.

MARCH 12

Finding Joy in Physical Activities

Bible Verse:

"The joy of the Lord is your strength." — Nehemiah 8:10 (MSG)

Commentary:

Finding joy in physical activities is essential for sustaining a healthy lifestyle. Nehemiah 8:10 reminds us that the joy of the Lord is our strength. When we engage in physical activities that we enjoy, we are more likely to stay committed and motivated. Joyful movement, whether walking, dancing, or playing a sport, boosts our mood, reduces stress, and fortifies our bodies. By finding activities that bring us happiness, we honor God with our bodies and cultivate a positive attitude that supports overall wellness and spiritual well-being.

Prayer:

Lord, help me find joy in physical activities that honor You. Fill me with Your strength and joy as I move and care for the body You have given me. Amen.

MARCH 13

Balancing Work and Rest

Bible Verse:

"Come to me, all you who are weary and burdened, and I will give you rest." — Matthew 11:28 (MSG)

Commentary:

Balancing work and rest is vital for maintaining physical, emotional, and spiritual fitness. Matthew 11:28 invites us to come to Jesus when we are weary, promising rest for our souls. It's important to work diligently and fulfill our responsibilities, but equally important to recognize when to rest and recharge. Finding balance ensures that we don't burn out and allows us to serve God and others like they deserve to be. By honoring both work and rest, we acknowledge our need for God's guidance and renewal, creating a rhythm that sustains us.

Prayer:

Heavenly Father, teach me to balance work and rest in a way that honors You. Help me to find strength in You and to rest when needed, trusting in Your care. Amen.

MARCH 14

Building a Supportive Wellness Community

Bible Verse:

"And let us consider how we may spur one another on toward love and good deeds." — Hebrews 10:24 (MSG)

Commentary:

Building a supportive wellness community encourages accountability and growth in our wellness journey. Hebrews 10:24 encourages us to spur one another on toward affection and good deeds. Surrounding ourselves with like-minded individuals who support and hearten us helps us stay motivated and committed to our health goals. A wellness community provides companionship, inspiration, and accountability, creating an environment where we can thrive physically, emotionally, and spiritually. By building and nurturing such a community, we foster a culture of care and encouragement that reflects God's love and promotes holistic well-being.

Prayer:

Lord, help me to build a supportive wellness community. Surround me with people who encourage and uplift me in my journey toward health and wellness. May we spur one another on in love and good deeds. Amen.

MARCH 15

The Spiritual Discipline of Fasting

Bible Verse:

"When you fast, do not look somber as the hypocrites do, for they disfigure their faces to show others they are fasting. Truly I tell you, they have received their reward in full." — Matthew 6:16 (MSG)

Commentary:

Fasting is a spiritual discipline that involves abstaining from food or certain activities to focus more intently on spirituality and God. Matthew 6:16 teaches us about the correct attitude to have when fasting—one of humility and sincerity. Fasting not only has spiritual benefits but also can positively impact physical health by allowing the body to detoxify and rest from constant digestion. It's a time to draw closer to God, seek His guidance, and promote self-control. By practicing fasting, we enhance both our spiritual and physical wellness, aligning our bodies and minds with God's will.

Prayer:

Heavenly Father, help me to fast with a sincere heart, seeking to grow closer to You. Teach me the discipline of self-control and help me honor You through fasting. Amen.

MARCH 16

Practicing Deep Breathing and Relaxation

Bible Verse:

"The Spirit of God has made me; the breath of the Almighty gives me life." — Job 33:4 (MSG)

Commentary:

Deep breathing and relaxation are simple yet powerful techniques for reducing stress and improving overall wellness. Job 33:4 reminds us that the breath of the Almighty gives us life. Practicing deep breathing helps calm the mind, reduce anxiety, and bring fresh air into the body, promoting relaxation and clarity. It's a reminder of the life-giving breath God provides and the importance of being present. Taking time to breathe deeply and relax allows us to reconnect with God, recenter our thoughts, and release tension, enhancing both physical and spiritual well-being.

Prayer:

Lord, help me to practice deep breathing and relaxation. Remind me of Your life-giving breath, and grant me peace and clarity as I focus on You. Amen.

MARCH 17

Embracing Silence and Solitude

Bible Verse:

"Be still, and know that I am God." — Psalm 46:10 (MSG)

Commentary:

Silence and solitude are essential for nurturing our spiritual and physical wellness. Psalm 46:10 encourages us to be still and know that God is present. Embracing silence and solitude allows us to withdraw from the noise and busyness of life, creating space to listen to God's voice. It helps reduce stress, improve focus, and renew our spirit. By taking time to be alone with God, we gain clarity and peace, deepening our relationship with Him. Regular practice of silence and solitude helps us cultivate inner calm and spiritual strength, guiding us toward a more balanced life.

Prayer:

Heavenly Father, teach me to embrace silence and solitude. Help me to find moments of stillness where I can listen to Your voice and know Your presence. Amen.

MARCH 18

The Healing Power of Nature

Bible Verse:

"The heavens declare the glory of God; the skies proclaim the work of his hands." — Psalm 19:1 (MSG)

Commentary:

Nature has a unique way of refreshing our minds and bodies, drawing us closer to God's creation. Psalm 19:1 reminds us that the heavens declare God's glory and His handiwork. Spending time outdoors helps reduce mental strain, improves mood, and enhances overall wellness. Being in nature allows us to witness God's creativity and majesty, fostering gratitude and peace. Whether walking in a park, sitting by a river, or hiking a trail, nature provides a sanctuary for reflection and renewal. Engaging with God's creation nurtures our spirits and promotes physical well-being.

Prayer:

Lord, thank You for the beauty of Your creation. Help me to find healing and refreshment in nature and to recognize Your glory in all that surrounds me. Amen.

MARCH 19

Journaling for Physical and Emotional Health

Bible Verse:

"Let us examine our ways and test them, and let us return to the Lord." — Lamentations 3:40 (MSG)

Commentary:

Journaling is a valuable tool for processing emotions and reflecting on our wellness journey. Lamentations 3:40 encourages us to examine our ways and return to the Lord. Writing down our thoughts, feelings, and experiences helps us gain insight into our emotions and behaviors, promoting emotional health and clarity. Journaling also allows us to track our progress, set goals, and express gratitude. By taking time for introspection, for instance, to write, we create a space for self-reflection and spiritual growth, helping us connect more deeply with God and understand ourselves better.

Prayer:

Heavenly Father, guide me as I journal and reflect on my journey. Help me to gain insight into my emotions and draw closer to You through this practice. Amen.

MARCH 20

Creative Outlets for Self-Care

Bible Verse:

"In the beginning, God created the heavens and the earth." — Genesis 1:1 (MSG)

Commentary:

Creative outlets are an excellent form of self-care, allowing us to express ourselves and reduce stress. Genesis 1:1 reminds us of God's creativity in creating the heavens and the earth. Engaging in creative and expressive activities like painting, writing, music, or crafting can bring joy and relaxation, enhancing our mental and emotional well-being. These activities help us connect with our inner selves and God's creativity, fostering a sense of accomplishment and fulfillment. By exploring creative outlets, we nurture our spirits, find a healthy balance, and enjoy the process of creation, reflecting the image of our Creator.

Prayer:

Lord, help me to explore creative outlets that bring joy and relaxation. May I reflect Your creativity in all I do, finding peace and fulfillment in the process. Amen.

MARCH 21

Self-Massage and Muscle Relief

Bible Verse:

"Come to me, all you who are weary and burdened, and I will give you rest." — Matthew 11:28 (MSG)

Commentary:

Self-massage is a simple yet effective way to relieve muscle tension and promote relaxation. Matthew 11:28 invites those who are weary to come to Jesus for rest. Just as Jesus offers spiritual rest, self-massage provides physical relief from stress and fatigue. By taking time to care for our bodies through massage, we can reduce pain, improve circulation, and boost relaxation. This practice allows us to honor the temple of the Holy Spirit, acknowledging the need for rest and restoration. Self-massage is a practical way to care for our physical well-being, encouraging us to find peace and rejuvenation.

Prayer:

Heavenly Father, thank You for the gift of rest and relief. Help me to care for my body and find peace in Your presence as I seek restoration. Amen.

MARCH 22

Honoring Our Bodies

Bible Verse:

"Do you not know that your bodies are temples of the Holy Spirit, who is in you, whom you have received from God? You are not your own." — 1 Corinthians 6:19 (NIV)

Commentary:

Our bodies are not just physical vessels but sacred temples housing the Holy Spirit. This profound truth calls us to view our physical health through a spiritual lens. When we care for our bodies—through proper diet, regular exercise, and adequate rest—we're not just improving our physical well-being but also honoring God. It's an act of stewardship, recognizing that our bodies are gifts entrusted to us by our Creator.

Prayer:

Loving Father, thank You for the gift of my body. Help me to honor it as Your temple, making choices that promote health and glorify You. Guide me in caring for myself as an act of worship. Amen.

MARCH 23

Nourishing Body and Soul

Bible Verse:

"So, whether you eat or drink or whatever you do, do it all for the glory of God." — 1 Corinthians 10:31 (NIV)

Commentary:

This verse reminds us that even our mundane activities, like eating and drinking, can be acts of worship. When we choose nutritious foods and consume a balanced diet, we're not just fueling our bodies—we're also honoring God's creation. Mindful eating becomes a spiritual practice, an opportunity to express gratitude for God's provision and to care for the body He's given us.

Prayer:

Gracious God, thank You for the nourishment You provide. Help me to make wise choices in my diet, seeing each meal as an opportunity to honor You and care for the body You've entrusted to me. Amen.

MARCH 24

The Blessing of Rest

Bible Verse:

"Come to me, all you who are weary and burdened, and I will give you rest." — Matthew 11:28 (NIV)

Commentary:

In our fast-paced world, rest is often overlooked or even seen as unproductive. Yet, Jesus Himself invites us to find rest in Him. Adequate sleep and periods of relaxation are crucial for our physical and spiritual well-being. When we prioritize rest, we're acknowledging our human limitations and trusting in God's sustaining power. It's in these moments of stillness and tranquility that we often find renewal for both body and soul.

Prayer:

Lord Jesus, thank You for the gift of rest. Help me to find balance in my life, trusting in Your promise of renewal. Teach me to rest in You, finding restoration for my body, mind, and spirit. Amen.

MARCH 25

Exercise as Worship

Bible Verse:

"For physical training is of some value, but godliness has value for all things, holding promise for both the present life and the life to come." — 1 Timothy 4:8 (NIV)

Commentary:

While this verse acknowledges the importance of spiritual growth, it also affirms the value of physical training. Regular exercise isn't just about maintaining our health or achieving a certain physique—it's about stewarding the strength and abilities God has given us. When we engage in physical activity with thankfulness and intentionality, it becomes an act of worship, celebrating the incredible way God has designed our bodies to move and function.

Prayer:

Heavenly Father, thank You for the ability to move and be active. Help me to see exercise as a form of worship, celebrating the strength and capabilities You've given me. Lord, guide me in maintaining a healthy balance of physical and spiritual disciplines. Amen.

MARCH 26

Mindfulness and God's Presence

Bible Verse:

"Be still, and know that I am God." — Psalm 46:10a (NIV)

Commentary:

In the midst of our busy lives, this verse calls us to stillness and awareness of God's presence. Practicing mindfulness—being fully present in the moment can be a powerful tool for both mental health and spiritual stability. When we take time to be still, breathe deeply, and center ourselves in God's presence, we nurture our emotional well-being and deepen our connection with our Creator.

Prayer:

God of peace, in the busyness of life, help me to find moments of stillness. Teach me to be mindful of Your presence in every moment, finding peace and renewal in the awareness of Your love. Amen.

MARCH 27

Holistic Healing

Bible Verse:

"Praise the Lord, my soul, and forget not all his benefits— who forgives all your sins and heals all your diseases." — Psalm 103:2-3 (NIV)

Commentary:

This psalm reminds us that God cares for our whole being—body, mind, and spirit. While we should absolutely seek medical care when needed, we can also trust in God's healing power. Taking care of our health involves both practical steps and faith. When we approach wellness holistically, addressing our physical needs while also nurturing our spiritual life, we open ourselves to the fullness of God's healing and spiritual refurbishment.

Prayer:

Healing God, thank You for Your care for every aspect of my being. Guide me in making choices that promote holistic health and help me to trust in Your healing power. May my pursuit of wellness draw me closer to You. Amen.

MARCH 28

The Joy of Movement

Bible Verse:

"You make known to me the path of life; you will fill me with joy in your presence, with eternal pleasures at your right hand." — Psalm 16:11 (NIV)

Commentary:

While this verse speaks of spiritual joy, it can also remind us of the joy found in physical movement. Our bodies are designed for motion, and engaging in activities we enjoy—whether it's dancing, hiking, swimming, or playing sports—can be a source of genuine pleasure. When we find joy in movement, we celebrate the incredible gift of our bodies and experience a taste of the abundant and blissful life God intends for us.

Prayer:

Joyful Creator, thank You for the gift of movement. Help me to find activities that bring me joy and keep me active. May the pleasure I find in moving my body be a reflection of the joy I find in Your presence. Amen.

MARCH 29

Stress Management and Trust

Bible Verse:

"Cast all your anxiety on him because he cares for you." — 1 Peter 5:7 (NIV)

Commentary:

Stress can significantly impact our physical health, affecting everything from our sleep to our immune system. This verse reminds us that we don't have to carry our burdens alone. Managing stress involves both practical techniques—like deep breathing, exercise, or time management—and spiritual practices of surrendering our worries to God. When we learn to leave our anxieties in His hands, we're not just improving our mental health but also deepening our trust in God's care.

Prayer:

Caring Father, I bring my stresses and anxieties to You. Teach me to trust You more fully, and guide me in managing stress in healthy ways. Help me to find peace in Your presence and strength in Your care. Amen.

MARCH 30

Community and Wellness

Bible Verse:

"And let us consider how we may spur one another on toward love and good deeds, not giving up meeting together." — Hebrews 10:24-25a (NIV)

Commentary:

While personal discipline is important for health, this verse reminds us of the power of community. Supportive relationships can greatly enhance our physical and spiritual well-being. Whether it's having an exercise buddy, sharing healthy meals with friends, or praying together, a community can provide encouragement, accountability, and joy in our wellness journey. As we care for ourselves, we're also called to support others in their health goals.

Prayer:

Lord of community, thank You for the gift of relationships. Help me to build and nurture connections that support my physical and spiritual health. Show me how to encourage others in their wellness journeys as well. Amen.

MARCH 31

Renewal and Transformation

Bible Verse:

"Therefore, we do not lose heart. Though outwardly we are wasting away, yet inwardly we are being renewed DAY by DAY." — 2 Corinthians 4:16 (NIV)

Commentary:

This verse offers a powerful standpoint on aging and physical limitations. While our bodies may face challenges over time, our inner selves can continue to grow and be renewed. This renewal comes through our relationship with God and the transforming power of His Spirit. As we care for our bodily health, we can also nurture our spiritual vitality, finding strength and purpose that transcends physical constraints.

Prayer:

Renewing God, thank You for the promise of inner renewal. As I care for my physical health, it continue to transform me from the inside out. Help me to find purpose and joy in every stage of life, growing ever closer to You. Amen.

WELCOME TO THE MONTH OF APRIL –
THEME: EMOTIONAL INTELLIGENCE AND RESILIENCE

APRIL 1

Understanding Emotional Intelligence

Bible Verse:

"A fool gives full vent to his spirit, but a wise man quietly holds it back." — Proverbs 29:11 (MSG)

Commentary:

Emotional intelligence is the ability to recognize, understand, and manage our emotions and the emotions of others. Proverbs 29:11 contrasts the wise person, who controls their emotions, with the fool, who gives full vent to them. Developing emotional intelligence helps us navigate relationships, make thoughtful decisions, and respond appropriately to the adversities of life. By cultivating emotional intelligence, we grow in wisdom, self-control, and, most importantly, empathy, allowing us to handle situations with grace and reflect Christ's love for others.

Prayer:

Lord, grant me wisdom to develop emotional intelligence. Help me to understand my emotions and respond to them with grace and self-control, reflecting Your love in all I do. Amen.

APRIL 2

Recognizing Your Emotions

Bible Verse:

"Search me, God, and know my heart; test me and know my anxious thoughts." — Psalm 139:23 (MSG)

Commentary:

Recognizing our emotions is the first step in building emotional awareness. Psalm 139:23 encourages us to invite God to search our hearts and reveal our innermost thoughts and feelings. By identifying our emotions, we become more self-aware and better equipped to manage them effectively. This practice helps us understand the root causes of our feelings, whether happiness, grief, anger, or fear. As we recognize our emotions, we can bring them before God, seeking His guidance and peace in every situation.

Prayer:

Heavenly Father, help me to recognize and understand my emotions. Search my heart and reveal any anxious thoughts. Guide me to manage my feelings with wisdom and grace. Amen.

APRIL 3

The Role of Emotions in Decision Making

Bible Verse:

"Trust in the Lord with all your heart and lean not on your own understanding." — Proverbs 3:5 (MSG)

Commentary:

Emotions play a significant role in our decision-making processes. Proverbs 3:5 advises us to trust in the Lord rather than rely solely on our understanding, which includes our emotions. While emotions can provide valuable insights, they can also cloud our judgment if not managed properly. By learning to discern when to trust our feelings and when to rely on God's wisdom, we make more balanced decisions. Incorporating prayer and sincerely seeking God's guidance helps us navigate our emotions and make choices that align with His will.

Prayer:

Lord, help me to understand the role of emotions in my decisions. Teach me to trust in You and seek Your wisdom, balancing my feelings with Your truth. Amen.

APRIL 4

Managing Negative Emotions

Bible Verse:

"In your anger do not sin; do not let the sun go down while you are still angry." — Ephesians 4:26 (MSG)

Commentary:

Managing negative emotions, such as anger, frustration, and sadness, is essential for emotional well-being. Ephesians 4:26 warns us not to let anger lead to sin or linger too long. Acknowledging our negative emotions without allowing them to control our actions helps us maintain peace and self-control. By bringing our feelings to God in prayer and seeking His guidance, we can find healthy ways to process and release these emotions, preventing them from causing harm to ourselves or others.

Prayer:

Heavenly Father, help me to manage my negative emotions in a way that honors You. Teach me to release anger and frustration through prayer and to find peace in Your presence. Amen.

APRIL 5

Positive Emotions

Bible Verse:

"Rejoice in the Lord always. I will say it again: Rejoice!" — Philippians 4:4 (MSG)

Commentary:

Cultivating positive emotions, such as joy, gratitude, and peace, enriches our lives and strengthens our emotional resilience. Philippians 4:4 encourages us to rejoice in the Lord always, regardless of our circumstances. By concentrating on the blessings God has given us and maintaining a grateful heart, we nurture positive emotions that uplift our spirits and improve our holistic well-being. Regularly practicing gratitude and finding joy in God's presence helps us develop a resilient, optimistic mindset that reflects His love and faithfulness.

Prayer:

Lord, help me to cultivate positive emotions in my life. Teach me to rejoice in You always and to maintain a grateful heart, finding joy in Your presence every DAY. Amen.

APRIL 6

Empathy: Understanding Others' Emotions

Bible Verse:

"Rejoice with those who rejoice; mourn with those who mourn." — Romans 12:15 (MSG)

Commentary:

Empathy is the ability to understand, relate to and share the feelings of others. Romans 12:15 encourages us to empathize by rejoicing with those who rejoice and mourning with those who mourn. Practicing empathy helps us build deeper, more meaningful relationships and fosters a spirit of compassion and kindness. By taking the time to listen and understand others' emotional experiences, we reflect Christ's love and support, offering comfort and encouragement to those in need. Each act of empathy creates a ripple effect, inspiring others to show kindness and compassion in their own lives while it fills us with greater fulfillment.

Prayer:

Heavenly Father, teach me to be empathetic and understanding toward others. Help me to share in their joys and sorrows, offering compassion and love as Christ does. Amen.

APRIL 7

The Impact of Emotions on Physical Health

Bible Verse:

"A cheerful heart is good medicine, but a crushed spirit dries up the bones." — Proverbs 17:22 (MSG)

Commentary:

Our emotions have a profound impact on our physical health. Proverbs 17:22 highlights that a cheerful heart promotes healing, while a crushed spirit can harm our physical well-being. Positive emotions like joy and gratitude can boost our immune system, lower stress, and improve overall health. Conversely, negative emotions such as chronic stress, anger, and sadness can lead to physical ailments. Understanding the connection between emotions and physical health encourages us to manage our feelings wisely and cultivate a positive, faith-filled mindset that promotes holistic wellness. This practice of nurturing positivity can inspire others to embark on their journeys towards physical and emotional well-being.

Prayer:

Lord, help me to recognize the impact of my emotions on my physical health. Teach me to cultivate a cheerful heart and to manage my feelings in a way that promotes wellness and honors You. Amen.

APRIL 8

Practicing Self-Control

Bible Verse:

"Like a city whose walls are broken through is a person who lacks self-control." — Proverbs 25:28 (MSG)

Commentary:

Practicing self-control is essential for managing our emotions and making wise decisions. Proverbs 25:28 compares a person without self-control to a city with broken walls, vulnerable to attack. Without self-control, we are susceptible to impulsive reactions and poor choices that can harm ourselves and others. By developing self-control, we strengthen our emotional resilience and learn to respond thoughtfully rather than react impulsively. This discipline helps us navigate challenges with grace and wisdom while also allowing us to honor God with our actions and maintain healthy relationships.

Prayer:

Lord, help me to practice self-control in all areas of my life. Teach me to manage my emotions and respond with wisdom and grace, reflecting Your love. Amen.

Finding Peace in Chaos

Bible Verse:

"He says, 'Be still, and know that I am God.'" — Psalm 46:10 (MSG)

Commentary:

Finding peace in the midst of chaos requires a calm mind and a steadfast trust in God. Psalm 46:10 invites us to be still and recognize God's sovereignty, even when life feels overwhelming. By focusing on God's presence and His control over every situation, we can remain calm and composed despite external turmoil. Practicing inner stillness and relying on God's peace allows us to navigate chaos with grace and confidence, trusting that He is in complete control and will guide us through any storm.

Prayer:

Heavenly Father, help me find peace in the midst of chaos. Teach me to be still and trust in Your presence, knowing that You are in control of every situation. Amen.

APRIL 10

Overcoming Emotional Overwhelm

Bible Verse:

"Come to me, all you who are weary and burdened, and I will give you rest." — Matthew 11:28 (MSG)

Commentary:

Overcoming emotional overwhelm involves seeking rest and refuge in God. Matthew 11:28 invites us to come to Jesus when we are weary and burdened, promising rest for our souls. When emotions become too much to bear, turning to God provides comfort and relief. By laying our burdens at His feet and trusting in His care, we can find peace and regain our emotional balance. Learning to surrender our overwhelm to God helps us manage our emotions effectively and rely on His strength in times of need. In His presence, we find the serenity that empowers us to face life's challenges with renewed hope.

Prayer:

Lord, help me to overcome emotional overwhelm by finding rest in You. Teach me to lay my burdens at Your feet and trust in Your care, knowing You will give me peace. Amen.

APRIL 11

Navigating Emotional Triggers

Bible Verse:

"A gentle answer turns away wrath, but a harsh word stirs up anger." — Proverbs 15:1 (MSG)

Commentary:

Navigating emotional triggers requires awareness and a calm response. Proverbs 15:1 highlights the power of a gentle answer to diffuse anger and prevent escalation. By recognizing situations or words that trigger strong emotions, we can prepare ourselves to respond thoughtfully rather than react impulsively. Practicing self-awareness and choosing gentle, measured responses helps us manage our triggers and maintain healthy relationships. This approach fosters peace and understanding, allowing us to handle challenging situations with grace. By embracing this mindset, we can create a safe space to have an affirmative dialogue within ourselves that will radiate peace and tranquility.

Prayer:

Heavenly Father, help me navigate my emotional triggers with wisdom and grace. Teach me to respond gently and maintain peace in all my interactions. Amen.

APRIL 12

Building Emotional Resilience

Bible Verse:

"We are hard pressed on every side, but not crushed; perplexed, but not in despair." — 2 Corinthians 4:8 (MSG)

Commentary:

Building emotional resilience is about developing the ability to bounce back from adversity. 2 Corinthians 4:8 reminds us that, although we face challenges, we are not defeated. Emotional resilience involves learning from difficult experiences and growing stronger through them. By trusting in God's strength and relying on His promises, we can endure hardships and emerge with greater faith and courage. Building resilience helps us face life's trials with confidence and hope, knowing that God is with us every step of the way.

Prayer:

Lord, help me build emotional resilience and strength through life's challenges. Teach me to trust in Your promises and rely on Your strength in all circumstances. Amen.

APRIL 13

The Power of Pause: Reflect Before Reacting

Bible Verse:

"Everyone should be quick to listen, slow to speak and slow to become angry." — James 1:19 (MSG)

Commentary:

The power of pause is an essential skill for emotional regulation. James 1:19 advises us to be quick to listen, slow to speak, and slow to become angry. Taking a moment to pause before reacting allows us to gather our thoughts and consider our responses carefully. This practice helps prevent impulsive reactions and encourages thoughtful communication. By reflecting before reacting, we can manage our emotions more efficiently, avoid misunderstandings, and promote healthier interactions with others.

Prayer:

Heavenly Father, teach me the power of pause. Help me to listen carefully, speak thoughtfully, and manage my emotions wisely, reflecting Your love in all my interactions. Amen.

APRIL 14

Developing Patience Through Emotional Challenges

Bible Verse:

"But if we hope for what we do not yet have, we wait for it patiently." — Romans 8:25 (MSG)

Commentary:

Developing patience through emotional challenges is crucial for emotional growth. Romans 8:25 encourages us to wait patiently for what we hope and pray for, even when faced with difficulties. Patience allows us to endure emotional challenges without becoming overwhelmed or discouraged. By trusting in God's timing and plan, we learn to navigate our emotions with grace and perseverance. Patience helps us grow in wisdom and strength, enabling us to face life's challenges with a calm and hopeful spirit.

Prayer:

Lord, help me develop patience through emotional challenges. Teach me to trust in Your timing and rely on Your strength, waiting patiently for Your promises. Amen.

APRIL 15

Enhancing Communication Skills

Bible Verse:

"Let your conversation be always full of grace, seasoned with salt, so that you may know how to answer everyone." — Colossians 4:6 (MSG)

Commentary:

Enhancing communication skills is crucial for building strong, healthy relationships. Colossians 4:6 encourages us to speak with grace, ensuring that our words are kind, respectful, and thoughtful. Effective communication involves actively listening, understanding others' perspectives, and expressing our thoughts clearly and respectfully. By practicing these skills, we create a positive environment where misunderstandings are minimized and connections are deepened. This approach fosters trust and empathy, allowing our relationships to thrive and reflect God's love.

Prayer:

Heavenly Father, help me to enhance my communication skills. Teach me to speak with grace and listen with understanding, building stronger, healthier relationships that honor You. Amen.

Building Trust and Emotional Safety

Bible Verse:

"Love always protects, always trusts, always hopes, always perseveres." — 1 Corinthians 13:7 (MSG)

Commentary:

Building trust and emotional safety is foundational for nurturing meaningful relationships. 1 Corinthians 13:7 highlights that love always protects and trusts, emphasizing the importance of creating a safe space for emotional expression. Trust is a form of emotional reliability that is built through consistent actions, honesty, and openness. By showing empathy and compassion, we provide a supportive environment where others feel valued and understood. Building trust encourages vulnerability and fosters deeper emotional connections, strengthening our relationships and reflecting God's unconditional love.

Prayer:

Lord, help me build trust and emotional safety in my relationships. Teach me to protect and support others with love and compassion, creating a space where they feel safe and valued. Amen.

Handling Conflict with Grace

Bible Verse:

"Blessed are the peacemakers, for they will be called children of God." — Matthew 5:9 (MSG)

Commentary:

Handling conflict with grace is essential for maintaining harmony in relationships. Matthew 5:9 calls peacemakers blessed, recognizing their role in fostering peace. Conflict is inevitable, but responding with grace and patience helps de-escalate tensions and promotes resolution. By approaching disagreements with a calm demeanor, listening actively, and seeking mutual understanding, we demonstrate Christ's love and maintain unity. Gracefully handling conflicts requires humility and a willingness to prioritize the relationship over being right.

Prayer:

Heavenly Father, teach me to handle conflict with grace. Help me to be a peacemaker, responding with patience and love and reflecting Your peace in all my interactions. Amen.

APRIL 18

Forgiveness: Letting Go of Emotional Baggage

Bible Verse:

"Bear with each other and forgive one another if any of you has a grievance against someone. Forgive as the Lord forgave you." — Colossians 3:13 (MSG)

Commentary:

Forgiveness is crucial for emotional healing and freedom. Colossians 3:13 instructs us to forgive as the Lord forgave us, highlighting the importance of letting go of grievances. Holding onto bitterness or resentment can weigh down our hearts and hinder our spiritual growth. By choosing to forgive, we release emotional baggage and open ourselves to God's healing. Forgiveness doesn't mean forgetting the hurt, but it does mean choosing peace over pain. It liberates us from the burden of anger and allows us to experience God's grace more fully.

Prayer:

Lord, help me to forgive as You have forgiven me. Teach me to let go of emotional baggage and embrace Your healing, finding peace and freedom in Your grace. Amen.

APRIL 19

Emotional Support: Being There for Others

Bible Verse:

"Carry each other's burdens, and in this way, you will fulfill the law of Christ." — Galatians 6:2 (MSG)

Commentary:

Providing emotional support to others is a powerful way to demonstrate love and compassion. Galatians 6:2 encourages us to carry each other's burdens, fulfilling Christ's law of love. Being there for others involves listening, offering comfort, and providing encouragement during difficult times. By showing empathy and understanding, we help others feel valued and supported. Emotional support strengthens our relations and creates a community where people feel connected and cared for, reflecting the love of Christ.

Prayer:

Heavenly Father, help me to be a source of emotional support for those around me. Teach me to carry others' burdens with compassion and love, fulfilling Your call to care for one another. Amen.

APRIL 20

The Role of Vulnerability in Relationships

Bible Verse:

"But if we walk in the light, as he is in the light, we have fellowship with one another." — 1 John 1:7 (MSG)

Commentary:

Vulnerability plays a vital role in deepening relationships and fostering trust. 1 John 1:7 emphasizes that walking in the light, or being open and honest, leads to true fellowship with others. Being vulnerable means sharing our authentic selves, including our fears, struggles, and joys. This openness allows for deeper emotional connections and mutual understanding. While vulnerability can feel risky, it creates a foundation for genuine relationships built on trust and love, reflecting God's desire for us to live in a cohesive community.

Prayer:

Lord, help me to embrace vulnerability in my relationships. Teach me to be open and honest, fostering deeper connections and reflecting Your love in all my interactions. Amen.

Setting Emotional Boundaries

Bible Verse:

"Above all else, guard your heart, for everything you do flows from it." — Proverbs 4:23 (MSG)

Commentary:

Setting emotional boundaries is essential for protecting our well-being and maintaining healthy relationships. Proverbs 4:23 urges us to guard our hearts, recognizing that our emotional health impacts every aspect of our lives. Emotional boundaries help us establish limits on what we will and will not accept from others, preventing emotional exhaustion and maintaining balance. By setting clear and healthy boundaries, we respect ourselves and others, fostering relationships based on mutual understanding and respect.

Prayer:

Heavenly Father, guide me in setting healthy emotional boundaries. Help me to guard my heart and maintain relationships that honor You and promote well-being. Amen.

APRIL 22

Learning from Emotional Setbacks

Bible Verse:

"Consider it pure joy, my brothers and sisters, whenever you face trials of many kinds, because you know that the testing of your faith produces perseverance." — James 1:2-3 (MSG)

Commentary:

Emotional setbacks can be hard to navigate through, but they offer opportunities for growth. James 1:2-3 encourages us to view trials with joy, knowing they build perseverance. When we face difficulties, we have the chance to learn more about ourselves, our emotions, our strength and our reliance on God. Reflecting on these experiences allows us to understand what triggers our reactions and how we can respond better in the future. By trusting in God's purpose, we can transform setbacks into stepping stones toward greater emotional strength and resilience.

Prayer:

Lord, help me learn from emotional setbacks and grow through challenges. Teach me to trust in Your purpose and use every experience to strengthen my faith and resilience. Amen.

APRIL 23

Gratitude as a Tool for Emotional Strength

Bible Verse:

"Give thanks in all circumstances, for this is God's will for you in Christ Jesus." — 1 Thessalonians 5:18 (MSG)

Commentary:

Gratitude is a powerful tool for building emotional strength. 1 Thessalonians 5:18 urges us to to grateful in all circumstances, recognizing that thankfulness shifts our focus from what we lack to what we have. By cultivating a thankful heart, we become more resilient, finding joy and hope even in difficult times. Gratitude helps us see God's blessings even in situations that don't make sense to us, fostering a positive outlook and strengthening our faith. Regularly practicing gratitude helps us stay grounded in God's love and maintain emotional balance.

Prayer:

Heavenly Father, help me to cultivate gratitude in every circumstance. Teach me to focus on Your blessings and to use thankfulness as a tool for emotional strength and resilience. Amen.

APRIL 24

Embracing Change with Emotional Flexibility

Bible Verse:

"For I know the plans I have for you," declares the Lord, "plans to prosper you and not to harm you, plans to give you hope and a future." — Jeremiah 29:11 (MSG)

Commentary:

Embracing change requires emotional flexibility and trust in God's plans. Jeremiah 29:11 reassures us that God's plans are for our own good, providing hope and a future. Change can be unsettling, but it also brings growth and new opportunities. By remaining emotionally flexible, we can adapt to life's transitions with contentment and resilience. Trusting in God's purpose allows us to face change with confidence, knowing that He is guiding us toward His best for our lives.

Prayer:

Lord, help me to embrace change with emotional flexibility and trust in Your plans. Teach me to adapt to life's transitions with grace, knowing You are leading me toward Your purpose. Amen.

APRIL 25

Fear and Anxiety

Bible Verse:

"For God has not given us a spirit of fear, but of power, love, and a sound mind." — 2 Timothy 1:7 (MSG)

Commentary:

Overcoming fear and anxiety requires faith in God's strength and promises. 2 Timothy 1:7 reminds us that God gives us a spirit of power, love, and a sound mind, not fear. When anxiety threatens to overwhelm us, we can choose to focus on God's truth and rely on His strength. By practicing deep breathing, prayer, and meditation on Scripture, we can calm our minds and find peace. Trusting in God's love and sovereignty helps us face our fears with courage and confidence. As we lean on Him, we allow faith to flourish even in the midst of uncertainty.

Prayer:

Heavenly Father, help me to overcome fear and anxiety by trusting in Your strength and promises. Teach me to rely on Your love and to find peace in Your presence. Amen.

Hope in Difficult Times

Bible Verse:

"May the God of hope fill you with all joy and peace as you trust in him, so that you may overflow with hope by the power of the Holy Spirit." — Romans 15:13 (MSG)

Commentary:

Finding hope in difficult times is essential for maintaining emotional resilience. Romans 15:13 reminds us that God is the source of hope, filling us with joy and peace as we trust in Him. Even in challenging situations, we can choose to focus on God's promises and remain hopeful. By leaning on God's strength and allowing the Holy Spirit to work within us, we can cultivate a sense of hope that transcends our circumstances. This hope sustains us through all trials in life and encourages us to keep moving forward.

Prayer:

Lord, help me to find hope in difficult times by trusting in Your promises. Fill me with joy and peace as I rely on Your strength, and may Your hope overflow in my heart. Amen.

APRIL 27

The Role of Faith in Emotional Resilience

Bible Verse:

"I can do all this through him who gives me strength." — Philippians 4:13 (MSG)

Commentary:

Faith plays a crucial role in building emotional resilience. Philippians 4:13 affirms that we can do all things through Christ, who gives us strength. When we face emotional challenges, our faith provides the foundation we need to persevere. By trusting in God's power and relying on His guidance, we can navigate life's ups and downs with unwavering courage and determination. Faith helps us stay anchored in God's promises, empowering us to overcome obstacles and emerge stronger.

Prayer:

Heavenly Father, strengthen my faith and help me to rely on Your power. Teach me to trust in You during emotional challenges and to build resilience through Your strength. Amen.

APRIL 28

Balancing Emotional and Rational Thinking

Bible Verse:

"The heart is deceitful above all things and beyond cure. Who can understand it?" — Jeremiah 17:9 (MSG)

Commentary:

Balancing emotional and rational thinking is crucial for wise decision-making. Jeremiah 17:9 warns that the heart can be deceitful, highlighting the need for discernment. Emotions provide valuable insight, but relying solely on them can lead to impulsive choices. By balancing our feelings with rational thought and seeking God's wisdom, we make decisions that honor Him. This balance helps us respond thoughtfully rather than react emotionally, harmonizing emotional intelligence and sound judgment in all situations.

Prayer:

Lord, help me to balance emotional and rational thinking in my decision-making. Teach me to seek Your wisdom and discernment, ensuring my choices honor You. Amen.

APRIL 29

Emotional Self-Care

Bible Verse:

"Come to me, all you who are weary and burdened, and I will give you rest." — Matthew 11:28 (MSG)

Commentary:

Practicing emotional self-care is vital for maintaining overall well-being. Matthew 11:28 invites us to come to Jesus for rest when we are weary and burdened. Emotional self-care involves taking time to nurture our mental and emotional health through activities that refresh and renew us. Whether it's spending time in prayer, journaling, or engaging in hobbies we enjoy, self-care helps us stay balanced and resilient. By prioritizing self-care, we honor God's call to rest and ensure we are equipped to serve Him and others.

Prayer:

Heavenly Father, teach me to practice emotional self-care and find rest in You. Help me to prioritize my well-being so I can serve You and others with strength and joy. Amen.

Reflecting on Emotional Growth

Bible Verse:

"Let us examine our ways and test them, and let us return to the Lord." — Lamentations 3:40 (MSG)

Commentary:

Reflecting on emotional growth helps us recognize progress and set goals for continued development. Lamentations 3:40 encourages us to examine our ways and return to the Lord. By taking time to reflect on our emotional journey, we can identify areas where we've grown and areas needing further improvement. This reflection fosters self-awareness and helps us align our lives more closely with God's will. By celebrating our progress and seeking God's guidance for future growth, we continue to mature emotionally and spiritually, creating a richer, more fulfilling life that reflects His love and purpose.

Prayer:

Lord, help me to reflect on my emotional growth and learn from my experiences. Teach me to seek Your guidance and continue growing in emotional and spiritual maturity. Amen.

WELCOME TO THE MONTH OF MAY – THEME: SPIRITUAL EXPLORATION AND GROWTH

MAY 1

The Nature of Faith

Bible Verse:

"Now faith is confidence in what we hope for and assurance about what we do not see." — Hebrews 11:1 (MSG)

Commentary:

Faith is the foundation of our relationship with God. Hebrews 11:1 defines faith as confidence in what we hope for and assurance about what we do not see. This means trusting in God's promises, even when we cannot see the full picture. Faith requires us to believe in God's goodness and His plans for us, no matter our circumstances. By exploring the nature of faith, we learn to trust God more profoundly, relying on His wisdom and timing in every aspect of our lives.

Prayer:

Lord, help me to understand and grow in my faith. Teach me to trust in Your promises and to rely on You, even when I cannot see the way forward. Amen.

MAY 2

Trusting in God's Promises

Bible Verse:

"For no matter how many promises God has made, they are 'Yes' in Christ." — 2 Corinthians 1:20 (MSG)

Commentary:

Trusting in God's promises is key to building a strong faith. 2 Corinthians 1:20 reminds us that all of God's promises are affirmed in Christ. This means we can have full confidence that what God has promised, He will fulfill. Trusting God requires us to hold onto His Word, believing that He is faithful and true. As we grow older in life, we often see the wisdom of his plans and promises unfolding before us. As we learn to trust in His promises, our faith is strengthened, and we grow more secure in His love and care for us.

Prayer:

Heavenly Father, help me to trust in Your promises. Strengthen my faith as I hold onto Your Word, believing that You are faithful and true. Amen.

MAY 3

The Power of Prayer

Bible Verse:

"The prayer of a righteous person is powerful and effective." — James 5:16 (MSG)

Commentary:

Prayer is a powerful tool for deepening our faith and a channel that connects us with God. James 5:16 teaches that the prayer of a righteous person is powerful and effective. Through prayer, we communicate with God, share our hearts, and seek His guidance. It's a way to express our trust in Him and our dependence on His strength. Regular prayer strengthens our relationship with God and helps us align our will with His. As we pray, our faith grows, and we experience God's presence more fully in our lives.

Prayer:

Lord, teach me the power of prayer. Help me to seek You daily and to grow closer to You through consistent communication. Amen.

MAY 4

Growing Through Scripture

Bible Verse:

"All Scripture is God-breathed and is useful for teaching, rebuking, correcting and training in righteousness." — 2 Timothy 3:16 (MSG)

Commentary:

Growing through Scripture is essential for spiritual development. 2 Timothy 3:16 reminds us that all Scripture is God-breathed and valuable for teaching and training in righteousness. By studying the Bible, we gain wisdom and understanding, learning more about God's character and His desires for us. Scripture provides guidance and correction, helping us stay firm on the path of righteousness. As we immerse ourselves in God's Word, our faith is strengthened, and we grow closer to Him.

Prayer:

Heavenly Father, help me to grow through Your Word. Teach me to study Scripture diligently and to apply its truths to my life. Amen.

MAY 5

Heart of Worship

Bible Verse:

"Come, let us bow down in worship, let us kneel before the Lord our Maker." — Psalm 95:6 (MSG)

Commentary:

Worship is an expression of our love and reverence for God. Psalm 95:6 invites us to bow down in worship and kneel before the Lord, recognizing His greatness. Cultivating a heart of worship means acknowledging God's worthiness and giving Him the honor He deserves. Worship deepens our relationship with God, reminding us of His power and sovereignty. Through worship, we express our gratitude, love, and devotion as well as our dependence, surrender and submission, drawing closer to God and growing in faith.

Prayer:

Lord, help me to cultivate a heart of worship. Teach me to honor You in all I do and to express my love for You through praise and adoration. Amen

MAY 6

Walking by Faith, Not by Sight

Bible Verse:

"For we live by faith, not by sight." — 2 Corinthians 5:7 (MSG)

Commentary:

Walking by faith, not by sight, means trusting in God even when we cannot see the outcome. 2 Corinthians 5:7 encourages us to live by faith, relying on God's guidance and wisdom rather than our understanding. This requires surrendering control and believing that God is working all things for our good. When we walk by faith, we demonstrate our trust in God's plans and vision, allowing Him to lead us. This not only deepens our relationship with God but also strengthens our faith in His provision.

Prayer:

Heavenly Father, teach me to walk by faith, not by sight. Help me to trust in Your plans and to rely on Your wisdom in all things. Amen.

MAY 7

The Role of Faith in Overcoming Doubt

Bible Verse:

"Immediately, the boy's father exclaimed, 'I do believe; help me overcome my unbelief!'" — Mark 9:24 (MSG)

Commentary:

Faith plays a crucial role in overcoming qualms, providing us with the assurance to confront doubts and uncertainties with confidence. Mark 9:24 captures a father's plea for help in believing, demonstrating that faith and doubt can coexist. When we experience 'doubt,' it's important to turn to God and ask for His help in strengthening our 'faith.' By focusing on God's promises and past faithfulness, we can overcome doubt and grow more confident in His love. Through prayer and Scripture, our faith is fortified, enabling us to trust God more fully and move beyond uncertainty.

Prayer:

Lord, help me to overcome my doubts and strengthen my faith. Teach me to trust in Your promises and rely on Your truth in all circumstances. Amen.

MAY 8

Recognizing God in Everyday Life

Bible Verse:

"The earth is the Lord's, and everything in it, the world, and all who live in it." — Psalm 24:1 (MSG)

Commentary:

Recognizing God in everyday life means seeing His hand in all things. Psalm 24:1 reminds us that the earth and everything in it belong to the Lord. This verse encourages us to see God's presence in every aspect of our daily lives, from the beauty of creation to the kindness of others. By looking for God in our surroundings and interactions, we become more aware of His constant presence and active role in our lives; this also fuels our faith in the two essential qualities of God– Omnipotence and Omnipresence. The awareness of this deepens our relationship with Him and enhances our spiritual growth.

Prayer:

Heavenly Father, help me recognize Your presence in my everyday life. Open my eyes to see Your hand in all things and to acknowledge Your goodness in every moment. Amen.

MAY 9

Practicing God's Presence

Bible Verse:

"Never will I leave you; never will I forsake you." — Hebrews 13:5 (MSG)

Commentary:

Practicing God's presence involves cultivating a constant awareness of His nearness. Hebrews 13:5 assures us that God will never leave or forsake us, reminding us of His unfailing presence. By intentionally focusing on God throughout the DAY, we can develop a deeper sense of His closeness. This practice includes praying, meditating, and acknowledging God's presence in our thoughts and actions. As we practice His presence, we grow more attuned to His guidance and comfort, experiencing greater peace and spiritual connection.

Prayer:

Lord, teach me to practice Your presence daily. Help me to remain aware of Your nearness and to live each moment with a conscious awareness of Your love. Amen.

MAY 10

Listening to God's Voice

Bible Verse:

"My sheep listen to my voice; I know them, and they follow me." — John 10:27 (MSG)

Commentary:

Listening to God's voice is crucial for spiritual growth and guidance. John 10:27 emphasizes that Jesus' followers know His voice and follow Him. To hear God's voice, we must quiet our hearts and minds, tuning in to His whispers through prayer, Scripture, and reflection. God often speaks through His Word, but He can also guide us through circumstances, other people, and the inner prompting of the Holy Spirit. By actively listening to God's voice and intentionally aligning ourselves with His will, we deepen our relationship with Him.

Prayer:

Heavenly Father, help me to listen to Your voice and follow Your guidance. Teach me to discern Your whispers and to respond with obedience and trust. Amen.

MAY 11

Finding God in Silence

Bible Verse:

"Be still, and know that I am God." — Psalm 46:10 (MSG)

Commentary:

Finding God in silence requires us to slow down and quiet our hearts. Psalm 46:10 calls us to be still and recognize God's sovereignty. In a world full of noise and distractions, it's essential to take time for silence and solitude, creating space and channel for God to speak to us. In these quiet moments, we can reflect on His Word, meditate on His character, and listen for His voice. By embracing silence, we become more attuned to God's presence, finding peace and clarity in His stillness.

Prayer:

Lord, teach me to find You in silence. Help me to be still and know that You are God, finding peace and clarity in Your presence. Amen.

MAY 12

Seeing God's Work in Nature

Bible Verse:

"The heavens declare the glory of God; the skies proclaim the work of his hands." — Psalm 19:1 (MSG)

Commentary:

Seeing God's work in nature allows us to witness His majesty and creativity. Psalm 19:1 tells us that the heavens declare God's glory and the skies proclaim His handiwork. Nature is a testament to God's power and beauty, revealing His character and love for His creation. By spending time in nature, we can uniquely connect with God, appreciating the intricate details of His work. The Earth and Universe are God's canvas, perfectly crafted to reflect His glory. Observing the world around us helps us to see God's presence more clearly and deepens our appreciation for His creation.

Prayer:

Heavenly Father, open my eyes to see Your work in nature. Help me to recognize Your glory and creativity in the world around me and to draw closer to You through Your creation. Amen.

MAY 13

Experiencing God's Grace

Bible Verse:

"For it is by grace you have been saved, through faith—and this is not from yourselves, it is the gift of God." — Ephesians 2:8 (MSG)

Commentary:

Experiencing God's grace is a transformative part of the Christian journey. Ephesians 2:8 reminds us that we are saved by grace through faith, emphasizing that grace is a gift from God. Grace is God's unmerited favor, extended to us despite our shortcomings. By recognizing and accepting God's grace, we are humbled and inspired to live in gratitude and obedience. Understanding grace deepens our relationship with God, reminding us of His love and mercy and encouraging us to extend grace to others.

Prayer:

Lord, help me to experience you gracefully. Teach me to live in gratitude for Your unmerited favor and to extend grace to those around me. Amen.

MAY 14

Inviting God into Your Daily Routine

Bible Verse:

"In all your ways submit to him, and he will make your paths straight." — Proverbs 3:6 (MSG)

Commentary:

Inviting God into your daily routine involves acknowledging Him in every aspect of life. Proverbs 3:6 encourages us to submit to God in all our ways, promising that He will direct our paths. By seeking God's guidance in our daily activities and decisions, we make Him a central part of our lives. This practice includes praying for His wisdom, reading Scripture, and being mindful of His presence throughout the DAY. As we invite God into our routines, we experience His guidance and grow closer to Him.

Prayer:

Heavenly Father, help me to invite You into every part of my daily routine. Teach me to seek Your guidance and to acknowledge Your presence in all I do. Amen.

Spiritual Disciplines

Bible Verse:

"Have nothing to do with godless myths and old wives' tales; rather, train yourself to be godly." — 1 Timothy 4:7 (MSG)

Commentary:

Understanding spiritual disciplines is crucial for developing a strong foundation in faith. 1 Timothy 4:7 encourages us to train ourselves to be godly, emphasizing the importance of discipline in spiritual growth. Spiritual disciplines, such as prayer, fasting, worship, and studying Scripture, help us draw closer to God and cultivate a deeper relationship with Him. By incorporating these practices into our daily lives, we build habits that strengthen our faith and foster spiritual maturity, allowing us to live more fully in alignment with God's will and words.

Prayer:

Lord, help me to understand and practice spiritual disciplines. Teach me to be disciplined in my faith, growing closer to You each DAY. Amen.

MAY 16

The Importance of Fellowship

Bible Verse:

"And let us consider how we may spur one another on toward love and good deeds, not giving up meeting together, as some are in the habit of doing but encouraging one another." — Hebrews 10:24-25 (MSG)

Commentary:

Fellowship is vital for spiritual growth and encouragement. Hebrews 10:24-25 urges us not to give up meeting together, highlighting the importance of community in fostering love and good deeds. Being in fellowship with other believers provides support, accountability, and opportunities to grow in faith together. Through shared experiences, worship, and study, we can strengthen each other and build a sense of belonging. The fellowship nurtures our spiritual foundation, helping us focus on God and His life purpose.

Prayer:

Heavenly Father, help me to value and seek fellowship with other believers. Teach me to encourage and support others in their faith journey, building a strong community in You. Amen.

MAY 17

Habit of Gratitude

Bible Verse:

"Give thanks to the Lord, for he is good; his love endures forever." — Psalm 107:1 (MSG)

Commentary:

A gratitude habit is essential for cultivating a positive and joyful spirit. Psalm 107:1 encourages us to thank the Lord for His goodness and enduring love. Practicing gratitude helps us focus on God's blessings and recognize His hand in our lives, fostering a heart of thankfulness. By making genuine expression of gratitude a habit, we become more aware of God's presence and provision, deepening our relationship with Him. A grateful heart enhances our spiritual foundation, leading to a more fulfilled and content life.

Prayer:

Lord, teach me to develop a habit of gratitude. Help me to recognize Your goodness and to give thanks in all circumstances, deepening my relationship with You. Amen.

MAY 18

Fasting as a Spiritual Discipline

Bible Verse:

"But when you fast, put oil on your head and wash your face, so that it will not be obvious to others that you are fasting, but only to your Father, who is unseen; and your Father, who sees what is done in secret, will reward you." — Matthew 6:17-18 (MSG)

Commentary:

Fasting is a powerful spiritual discipline that helps us focus on God and seek His will. Matthew 6:17-18 instructs us to fast privately and sincerely, emphasizing the importance of a pure heart in fasting. By abstaining from food or other distractions, we create space to pray, meditate, and listen to God more attentively. Fasting is a way to humble ourselves before God, limit our greed for worldly desires, express our dependence on Him, and grow spiritually. This practice strengthens our spiritual foundation, drawing us closer to God and enhancing our awareness of His presence.

Prayer:

Heavenly Father, help me to understand and practice fasting as a spiritual discipline. Teach me to seek You earnestly and to grow closer to You through this practice. Amen.

MAY 19

The Power of Confession

Bible Verse:

"If we confess our sins, he is faithful and just and will forgive us our sins and purify us from all unrighteousness." — 1 John 1:9 (MSG)

Commentary:

Confession is a vital aspect of spiritual growth and healing. 1 John 1:9 assures us that if we confess our sins, God is faithful and just to forgive us and purify us from all unrighteousness. Confession allows us to acknowledge our mistakes, seek God's forgiveness, and experience His grace. By regularly confessing our sins, we maintain a healthy relationship with God and avoid the burden of unconfessed wrongdoing. This practice helps us stay humble and dependent on God's mercy, strengthening our spiritual foundation and drawing us closer to Him.

Prayer:

Lord, help me to practice confession regularly. Teach me to come before You with a humble heart, seeking Your forgiveness and grace, and maintaining a strong relationship with You. Amen.

MAY 20

Meditating on God's Word

Bible Verse:

"Keep this Book of the Law always on your lips; meditate on it DAY and night, so that you may be careful to do everything written in it." — Joshua 1:8 (MSG)

Commentary:

Meditating on God's Word is essential for spiritual growth and understanding. Joshua 1:8 instructs us to meditate on Scripture DAY and night, emphasizing the importance of constant reflection on God's Word. Meditation allows us to internalize God's teachings, gain wisdom, and apply His principles to our lives. By spending time pondering Scripture, we deepen our knowledge of God and align our hearts with His will. This practice strengthens our spiritual foundation, helping us grow in faith and live more fully according to God's desires. As we meditate on His Word, we may find clarity in our decisions, comfort in our struggles, and inspiration for our daily lives.

Prayer:

Heavenly Father, teach me to meditate on Your Word daily. Help me to internalize Your teachings and to apply them to my life, growing in wisdom and faith. Amen.

MAY 21

Embracing Sabbath Rest

Bible Verse:

"Then he said to them, 'The Sabbath was made for man, not man for the Sabbath.'" — Mark 2:27 (MSG)

Commentary:

Embracing Sabbath rest is crucial for spiritual renewal and well-being. Mark 2:27 reminds us that the Sabbath was made for our benefit, not as a burden. Taking time to rest and focus on God helps us recharge physically, mentally, and spiritually. Sabbath rest allows us to step away from the commotions of life and spend time in worship, reflection, and connection with God. By honoring the Sabbath, we acknowledge our dependence on God and create space for Him to restore our souls, strengthening our spiritual foundation.

Prayer:

Lord, help me to embrace Sabbath rest and to prioritize time with You. Teach me to find renewal in Your presence and to honor the Sabbath as a gift from You. Amen.

MAY 22

Finding Strength in Trials

Bible Verse:

"Consider it pure joy, my brothers and sisters, whenever you face trials of many kinds, because you know that the testing of your faith produces perseverance." — James 1:2-3 (MSG)

Commentary:

Finding strength in trials is essential for spiritual growth. James 1:2-3 encourages us to consider trials as opportunities for joy, knowing that they produce perseverance. Challenges test our faith and develop our spiritual endurance, helping us grow stronger and more resilient. By trusting God and relying on His strength, we can face difficulties with confidence and grace. Embracing trials as opportunities for personal evolution allows us to deepen our relationship with God and evolve more steadfastly in our faith.

Prayer:

Lord, help me find strength in trials. Teach me to trust You in all circumstances and to embrace challenges as opportunities for growth in my faith. Amen.

MAY 23

The Role of Suffering in Spiritual Growth

Bible Verse:

"Not only so, but we also glory in our sufferings, because we know that suffering produces perseverance; perseverance, character; and character, hope." — Romans 5:3-4 (MSG)

Commentary:

Suffering plays a significant role in spiritual growth. Romans 5:3-4 tells us that suffering produces perseverance, character, and hope. Through suffering, we learn to depend on God and develop qualities like patience, humility, and compassion. Painful experiences can draw us closer to God, helping us to understand His love and grace more deeply. By enduring suffering with faith, we allow God to mold us into His likeness, strengthening our character and deepening our hope in Him.

Prayer:

Heavenly Father, help me to see the purpose in suffering. Teach me to rely on You through difficult times and to grow in character and hope through my struggles. Amen.

Persevering in Faith

Bible Verse:

"Blessed is the one who perseveres under trial because, having stood the test, that person will receive the crown of life that the Lord has promised to those who love him." — James 1:12 (MSG)

Commentary:

Persevering in faith is crucial for spiritual maturity. James 1:12 assures us that those who persevere under trial will receive the crown of life. Perseverance requires steadfastness, patience, and unwavering trust in God's promises. When we face challenges, it's essential to remain faithful, trusting that God is working for our good. Persevering in faith reinforces our relationship with God and prepares us for the rewards He has promised. It helps us grow spiritually, developing a deeper reliance on His strength and guidance.

Prayer:

Lord, teach me to persevere in faith through every trial. Help me to remain steadfast, trusting in Your promises and relying on Your strength in all circumstances. Amen.

MAY 25

Trusting God's Plan in Uncertainty

Bible Verse:

"Trust in the Lord with all your heart and lean not on your own understanding; in all your ways submit to him, and he will make your paths straight." — Proverbs 3:5-6 (MSG)

Commentary:

Trusting God's plan in times of uncertainty is vital for spiritual growth. Proverbs 3:5-6 encourages us to trust in the Lord with all our hearts, leaning not on our own understanding. When life is uncertain, it's easy to become apprehensive or fearful, but trusting God means surrendering our worries and believing that He is in control. By submitting to God's will and relying on His guidance, we find peace and direction. Trusting God's plan deepens our faith and helps us grow in confidence in His perfect wisdom.

Prayer:

Heavenly Father, help me trust Your plan, especially in uncertain times. Teach me to rely on Your wisdom and submit to Your guidance, knowing that You will make my paths straight. Amen.

MAY 26

Learning Patience Through Waiting

Bible Verse:

"But if we hope for what we do not yet have, we wait for it patiently." — Romans 8:25 (MSG)

Commentary:

Learning patience through waiting is an essential aspect of spiritual growth. Romans 8:25 reminds us that waiting patiently for what we hope for strengthens our character and faith. Patience is developed when we trust God's timing, believing that He knows what is best for us. Waiting teaches us to be content with God's provision and to remain hopeful, even when our desires are not immediately fulfilled. By practicing patience, we grow in our ability to trust God and rely on His divine wisdom and perfect timing for our lives.

Prayer:

Lord, teach me to learn patience through waiting. Help me to trust in Your timing and to remain hopeful, knowing that Your plans for me are good. Amen.

MAY 27

The Refining Power of Difficulties

Bible Verse:

"These have come so that the proven genuineness of your faith—of greater worth than gold, which perishes even though refined by fire—may result in praise, glory, and honor when Jesus Christ is revealed." — 1 Peter 1:7 (MSG)

Commentary:

Difficulties have a refining power that purifies and strengthens our faith. 1 Peter 1:7 compares the testing of our faith to the refining of gold, highlighting its value. Challenges and hardships can strip away our reliance on worldly things and draw us closer to God. Through difficulties, our faith is tested and proven genuine, resulting in praise and honor when we remain steadfast. By embracing trials as polishing tools, we allow God to shape our character and deepen our relationship with Him.

Prayer:

Heavenly Father, help me see the refining power of difficulties. Teach me to embrace challenges as opportunities to purify my faith and grow closer to You. Amen.

MAY 28

Growing in Humility Through Hardships

Bible Verse:

"Humble yourselves, therefore, under God's mighty hand, that he may lift you up in due time." — 1 Peter 5:6 (MSG)

Commentary:

Hardships can help us grow in humility by reminding us of our dependence on God. 1 Peter 5:6 encourages us to humble ourselves under God's mighty hand, trusting that He will lift us up in due time. When we face difficulties, we often realize our limitations and need for God's strength and guidance. Embracing humility during hardships allows us to submit to God's will and rely on His grace. Growing in humility amplifies our relationship with God, helping us to recognize His sovereignty and trust in His provision.

Prayer:

Lord, help me to grow in humility through hardships. Teach me to rely on Your strength and submit to Your will, trusting that You will lift me up in due time. Amen.

MAY 29

God's Unconditional Love

Bible Verse:

"But God demonstrates his own love for us in this: While we were still sinners, Christ died for us." — Romans 5:8 (MSG)

Commentary:

Understanding God's unconditional love is foundational for spiritual growth. Romans 5:8 reminds us that God's love for us is so profound that He sent His Son to die for us even while we were still sinners. This unconditional love is not based on our actions but on God's nature. Recognizing this love helps us appreciate the depth of God's grace and mercy. It encourages us to live in gratitude, knowing we are cherished beyond measure. Embracing God's love renovates our hearts and inspires us to love others in the same way.

Prayer:

Heavenly Father, help me to understand the depth of Your unconditional love. Teach me to live in gratitude for Your grace and to reflect Your love to those around me. Amen.

MAY 30

Discovering Your God-Given Purpose

Bible Verse:

"For we are God's handiwork, created in Christ Jesus to do good works, which God prepared in advance for us to do." — Ephesians 2:10 (MSG)

Commentary:

Discovering your God-given purpose is essential for a fulfilling spiritual life. Ephesians 2:10 tells us that we are God's handiwork, created to do good works that He prepared in advance. Each of us has a unique purpose that God has designed for us. Understanding this purpose involves seeking God's guidance and aligning our lives with His will. By discovering and living out our purpose, we honor God and contribute to His kingdom. Embracing our God-given purpose brings joy and fulfillment, knowing we are walking in the path He has set for us.

Prayer:

Lord, help me discover my God-given purpose. Teach me to seek Your guidance and to live out the good works You have prepared for me, bringing glory to Your name. Amen.

MAY 31

Living Out Your Faith Daily

Bible Verse:

"In the same way, let your light shine before others, that they may see your good deeds and glorify your Father in heaven." — Matthew 5:16 (MSG)

Commentary:

Living out your faith daily is about reflecting God's love and character in everything you do. Matthew 5:16 encourages us to let our light shine before others so they may see our good deeds and glorify God. Our actions, words, and attitudes should demonstrate the transformation God has worked in our hearts. By living out our faith, we become a testament to God's grace and power. This daily commitment to living for Christ not only strengthens our relationship with God but also impacts those around us, drawing them closer to Him.

Prayer:

Heavenly Father, help me to live out my faith daily. Teach me to reflect Your love and grace in all I do so others may see You through my actions and glorify Your name. Amen.

WELCOME TO THE MONTH OF JUNE –
THEME: RELATIONSHIP AND SOCIAL CONNECTIONS

JUNE 1

The Foundation of Healthy Relationships

Bible Verse:

"A friend loves at all times, and a brother is born for a time of adversity." — Proverbs 17:17 (MSG)

Commentary:

Healthy relationships are built on love, trust, and mutual respect. Proverbs 17:17 highlights the enduring nature of a true friend and the support of a sibling in difficult times. Building a strong foundation in relationships requires intentional and reciprocal effort, open communication, and a commitment to understanding each other. When we prioritize these qualities, our relationships become sources of strength and joy. By focusing on the core principles of healthy connections, we create bonds that withstand challenges and bring lasting fulfillment.

Prayer:

Lord, help me to build healthy relationships rooted in love, trust, and respect. Teach me to be a good friend and a supportive companion in all circumstances. Amen.

JUNE 2

The Role of Trust in Relationships

Bible Verse:

"Trust in the Lord with all your heart and lean not on your own understanding." — Proverbs 3:5 (MSG)

Commentary:

Trust is a cornerstone of any meaningful relationship. Proverbs 3:5 reminds us to trust in the Lord, which can also be applied to our interactions with others. Trust involves being reliable, honest, and keeping promises. It requires us to believe in the good intentions of others and to be trustworthy ourselves. When trust is present, relationships thrive, and communication flows freely. Building trust requires time, but it is indispensable for creating strong, lasting connections with others.

Prayer:

Heavenly Father, help me to be trustworthy in all my relationships. Teach me to build trust through honesty and integrity, reflecting Your faithfulness. Amen.

JUNE 3

Communication: The Key to Connection

Bible Verse:

"Let your conversation be always full of grace, seasoned with salt, so that you may know how to answer everyone." — Colossians 4:6 (MSG)

Commentary:

Effective communication is vital for connecting with others. Colossians 4:6 encourages us to speak with grace, ensuring our words are kind and thoughtful. Good communication involves both speaking and listening, sharing openly while being receptive to others. It helps prevent misunderstandings and builds deeper connections. By practicing active listening and expressing ourselves clearly and politely, we foster an environment of trust and understanding. Prioritizing effective communication strengthens relationships and helps us grow closer to those around us.

Prayer:

Lord, guide me to communicate with grace and kindness. Help me to listen attentively and speak thoughtfully, building stronger connections with those I love. Amen.

JUNE 4

The Importance of Listening

Bible Verse:

"My dear brothers and sisters, take note of this: Everyone should be quick to listen, slow to speak and slow to become angry." — James 1:19 (MSG)

Commentary:

Listening is a crucial aspect of building strong relationships. James 1:19 advises us to listen quickly and speak slowly, highlighting the importance of understanding others before responding. Active listening involves giving our full attention, acknowledging feelings, and showing empathy. When we listen well, we demonstrate respect and create a safe space for an open dialogue. By making an effort to truly hear others, we deepen our connections and foster trust in our relationships.

Prayer:

Heavenly Father, teach me to be a good listener. Help me to be patient and attentive, showing empathy and understanding in my conversations. Amen.

JUNE 5

Setting Healthy Boundaries

Bible Verse:

"Above all else, guard your heart, for everything you do flows from it." — Proverbs 4:23 (MSG)

Commentary:

Setting healthy boundaries is essential for maintaining balanced relationships. Proverbs 4:23 urges us to guard our hearts, recognizing that our well-being affects all areas of life. Boundaries help protect our emotional, mental, and spiritual health by defining limits on what we accept from others. They ensure that we maintain respect and mutual understanding in our interactions. Establishing clear and healthy boundaries allows us to build vigorous, respectful relationships where both parties feel heard, valued and understood.

Prayer:

Lord, help me to set healthy boundaries in my relationships. Teach me to guard my heart and to create a balance that honors both myself and others. Amen.

JUNE 6

The Power of Encouragement

Bible Verse:

"Therefore encourage one another and build each other up, just as, in fact, you are doing." — 1 Thessalonians 5:11 (MSG)

Commentary:

Encouragement is a powerful tool for strengthening relationships. 1 Thessalonians 5:11 calls us to encourage and build one another up. Positive words and actions can uplift spirits, provide motivation, and create a supportive environment. When we encourage others, we affirm their worth and potential, fostering a sense of belonging and confidence. Practicing encouragement habitually helps cultivate a culture of positivity and strengthens the bonds we share with those around us.

Prayer:

Heavenly Father, help me to be a source of encouragement for others. Teach me to uplift and build those around me, spreading Your love and positivity. Amen.

JUNE 7

Balancing Give and Take

Bible Verse:

"Do to others as you would have them do to you."—
Luke 6:31 (MSG)

Commentary:

Balancing give and take is vital for maintaining healthy relationships. Luke 6:31 encourages us to treat others as we wish to be treated, emphasizing the importance of mutual respect and fairness. Relationships flourish when there is a balance of giving and receiving, ensuring that both parties reciprocate value and appreciation towards one another. By being generous with our time, energy, and support while also allowing others to give, we create strong, reciprocal connections that are mutually fulfilling.

Prayer:

Lord, help me to balance giving and receiving in my relationships. Teach me to be generous and to appreciate the kindness of others, fostering healthy, reciprocal connections. Amen.

JUNE 8

Love Languages

Bible Verse:

"Dear children, let us not love with words or speech but with actions and in truth." — 1 John 3:18 (MSG)

Commentary:

Understanding love languages is key to expressing and receiving love effectively. 1 John 3:18 reminds us that love should be demonstrated through actions and truth, not just words. Each person has a unique way of feeling loved, known as their love language, which may include words of affirmation, acts of service, receiving gifts, quality time, or physical touch. By learning and understanding the love languages of those around us, we can show love in ways that resonate deeply with them, strengthening our relationships and fostering meaningful connections.

Prayer:

Lord, help me to understand the love languages of those around me. Teach me to express love in ways that truly speak to their hearts and build stronger relationships. Amen.

JUNE 9

Practicing Empathy

Bible Verse:

"Rejoice with those who rejoice; mourn with those who mourn." — Romans 12:15 (MSG)

Commentary:

Practicing empathy is essential for building deep and meaningful relationships. Romans 12:15 encourages us to rejoice with those who rejoice and mourn with those who mourn, showing empathy in all circumstances. Empathy involves putting ourselves in another person's shoes– feeling their emotions and understanding their experiences from their perspectives. By practicing empathy, we demonstrate compassion and support, helping others feel seen and valued. This practice strengthens our connections and builds trust, creating a more loving and supportive community.

Prayer:

Heavenly Father, teach me to practice empathy in my relationships. Help me to understand the feelings of others and to offer genuine support and compassion. Amen.

The Role of Compassion in Relationships

Bible Verse:

"Finally, all of you, be like-minded, be sympathetic, love one another, be compassionate and humble." — 1 Peter 3:8 (MSG)

Commentary:

Compassion is a vital component of strong, healthy relationships. 1 Peter 3:8 calls us to be compassionate and humble, fostering unity and love. Compassion involves being sensitive to the needs and feelings of others and responding with kindness and care. By showing compassion, we build an environment of understanding and support where people feel valued and respected. Practicing compassion in our relationships encourages openness and vulnerability, leading to deeper, more meaningful connections.

Prayer:

Lord, help me to be compassionate in my relationships. Teach me to respond to others with kindness and care, reflecting Your love in all I do. Amen.

JUNE 11

Forgiving Others

Bible Verse:

"Be kind and compassionate to one another, forgiving each other, just as in Christ God forgave you." — Ephesians 4:32 (MSG)

Commentary:

Forgiving others is essential for maintaining healthy and resilient relationships. Ephesians 4:32 urges us to forgive as God forgave us in Christ, highlighting the importance of grace and mercy. Forgiveness allows us to let go of resentment and bitterness, freeing us to move forward in love. It fosters healing and reconciliation, strengthening our connections with others. By choosing to forgive, we emulate God's love and grace, creating an environment where relationships can thrive and grow.

Prayer:

Heavenly Father, teach me to forgive others as You have forgiven me. Help me to release any bitterness and extend grace, fostering healing and unity in my relationships. Amen.

JUNE 12

Expressing Gratitude in Relationships

Bible Verse:

"Give thanks in all circumstances, for this is God's will for you in Christ Jesus." — 1 Thessalonians 5:18 (MSG)

Commentary:

Expressing gratitude is a powerful way to strengthen relationships. 1 Thessalonians 5:18 encourages us to give thanks in all circumstances, recognizing the blessings in our lives. By expressing gratitude to those around us, we acknowledge their contributions and show appreciation for their presence. This practice fosters a positive atmosphere and reinforces the value of our relationships. Gratitude helps build mutual respect and admiration, deepening our bonds and promoting a reinforced sense of belonging.

Prayer:

Lord, help me to express gratitude in my relationships. Teach me to recognize the blessings others bring into my life and to show appreciation for their love and support. Amen.

JUNE 13

Managing Conflict Gracefully

Bible Verse:

"A gentle answer turns away wrath, but a harsh word stirs up anger." — Proverbs 15:1 (MSG)

Commentary:

Managing conflict gracefully is crucial for maintaining harmony in relationships. Proverbs 15:1 highlights the power of a gentle response in diffusing anger and tension. Conflicts are inevitable, but how we handle them makes a significant difference. Approaching disagreements with a calm and open heart allows for constructive dialogue and resolution. By choosing to respond with kindness and understanding, we prevent escalation and foster a spirit of reconciliation, consolidating our relationships and promoting peace.

Prayer:

Heavenly Father, teach me to manage conflict with grace and wisdom. Help me to respond gently and to seek resolution in a way that honors You and strengthens my relationships. Amen.

Building Emotional Intimacy

Bible Verse:

"Carry each other's burdens, and in this way, you will fulfill the law of Christ."— Galatians 6:2 (MSG)

Commentary:

Building emotional intimacy involves sharing our hearts and supporting one another through life's challenges. Galatians 6:2 encourages us to share each other's burdens, fostering a deep sense of connection and empathy. Emotional intimacy is cultivated through vulnerability, open communication, and mutual support. By being present and available for one another, we create a safe space for sharing feelings and experiences. This deepens our relationships, building trust and closeness that reflects the love of Christ.

Prayer:

Lord, help me to build emotional intimacy in my relationships. Teach me to share openly and to support others with compassion and understanding, creating a strong bond of trust and love. Amen.

JUNE 15

The Importance of Family Relationships

Bible Verse:

"Honor your father and your mother, so that you may live long in the land the Lord your God is giving you." — Exodus 20:12 (MSG)

Commentary:

Family relationships play a crucial role in shaping our values, beliefs, and character. Exodus 20:12 emphasizes the importance of honoring our parents and recognizing the foundational role of family in our lives. By valuing and nurturing our family connections, we create an environment of love, support, and growth. Healthy family relationships provide a safe space for learning, encouragement, and spiritual development. Strengthening these bonds nurtures a sense of belonging and helps us grow into the people God created us to be.

Prayer:

Heavenly Father, help me to value and strengthen my family relationships. Teach me to honor my parents and to nurture the bonds that connect us, reflecting Your love and grace. Amen.

JUNE 16

Honoring Your Parents

Bible Verse:

"Children, obey your parents in the Lord, for this is right." — Ephesians 6:1 (MSG)

Commentary:

Honoring our parents is a fundamental aspect of building strong family bonds. Ephesians 6:1 instructs children to obey their parents as a righteous act, reflecting God's design for family structure. Honoring our parents goes beyond obedience; it involves showing respect, gratitude, and love. By acknowledging their sacrifices and efforts in our upbringing and appreciating their guidance, we strengthen our family relationships. This respect fosters a harmonious environment where everyone feels valued and understood, enhancing the overall well-being of the family unit.

Prayer:

Lord, help me to honor my parents in all I do. Teach me to show respect, love, and gratitude, strengthening our relationship and reflecting Your grace. Amen.

Building Strong Sibling Relationships

Bible Verse:

"How good and pleasant it is when God's people live together in unity!" — Psalm 133:1 (MSG)

Commentary:

Building strong sibling relationships is essential for family unity and harmony. Psalm 133:1 celebrates the beauty of living together in unity, highlighting the joy that comes from strong family bonds. Siblings can be our first friends, providing companionship, support, and understanding. By fostering open communication, mutual respect, and shared experiences, we can build lasting connections with our siblings. Strong sibling relationships contribute to a supportive family environment where love and unity prevail.

Prayer:

Heavenly Father, help me to build strong relationships with my siblings. Teach me to communicate openly, respect each other, and foster unity, creating a loving and supportive family environment. Amen.

JUNE 18

Nurturing Your Children's Hearts

Bible Verse:

"Start children off on the way they should go, and even when they are old, they will not turn from it."
— Proverbs 22:6 (MSG)

Commentary:

Nurturing your children's hearts is vital for their emotional and spiritual development. Proverbs 22:6 emphasizes the importance of guiding children on the right path, ensuring they grow up with strong values and faith. By being attentive, supportive, and loving, we can help our children develop a deep sense of security and self-worth. Encouraging their spiritual growth through prayer, Bible study, and positive role modeling lays a solid foundation for their faith. Nurturing our children's hearts helps them grow into confident, compassionate, and responsible individuals who love and serve God.

Prayer:

Lord, help me to nurture my children's hearts with love and wisdom. Teach me to guide them in Your ways, helping them grow into faithful and compassionate individuals. Amen.

The Role of Faith in Family

Bible Verse:

"But as for me and my household, we will serve the Lord." — Joshua 24:15 (MSG)

Commentary:

Faith plays a pivotal role in strengthening family bonds and guiding the family's direction. Joshua 24:15 declares the commitment to serve the Lord as a family, emphasizing the importance of shared faith in building a strong household. By fostering a spiritual atmosphere at home, families can grow together in their relationship with God. Regular prayers, recitation, and understanding of the Bible, along with worship as a family, create opportunities for spiritual growth and unity. A shared faith helps families navigate challenges with grace and reinforces the values and beliefs that hold them together.

Prayer:

Heavenly Father, help me to cultivate a strong faith within my family. Teach us to serve You together and to grow in unity and love, strengthening our bond through our shared commitment to You. Amen.

Creating Family Traditions

Bible Verse:

"Tell it to your children, and let your children tell it to their children, and their children to the next generation." — Joel 1:3 (MSG)

Commentary:

Creating family traditions is a meaningful way to build strong bonds and pass down values. Joel 1:3 encourages us to share our stories and experiences with future generations, fostering a sense of continuity and belonging. Traditions provide a sense of identity and create lasting memories that strengthen family ties. Whether it's celebrating holidays, sharing meals, or engaging in regular family activities, traditions help reinforce the values and beliefs that define the family. By establishing and maintaining traditions, families create a rich tapestry of shared experiences that nurture connection and unity.

Prayer:

Lord, help me to create meaningful traditions that strengthen my family. Teach us to cherish these moments and to pass down our values and faith to future generations. Amen.

JUNE 21

Dealing with Family Conflict

Bible Verse:

"Make every effort to live in peace with everyone and to be holy; without holiness, no one will see the Lord." — Hebrews 12:14 (MSG)

Commentary:

Dealing with family conflict requires patience, understanding, and a commitment to peace. Hebrews 12:14 urges us to make every effort to live in peace with everyone, emphasizing the importance of harmony in relationships. Conflicts are natural in any family, but how we handle them can strengthen or weaken bonds. Approaching conflicts with a calm demeanor, open communication, and a willingness to forgive fosters a peaceful environment and harnesses love. By prioritizing reconciliation and seeking resolution, we maintain healthy, affectionate relationships that reflect God's love and grace.

Prayer:

Heavenly Father, help me to deal with family conflicts with grace and wisdom. Teach me to seek peace and understanding, fostering a harmonious and loving home. Amen.

JUNE 22

The Value of True Friendship

Bible Verse:

"A friend loves at all times, and a brother is born for a time of adversity." — Proverbs 17:17 (MSG)

Commentary:

True friendship is a gift that brings joy, support, and companionship. Proverbs 17:17 highlights the constancy and reliability of a true friend who loves at all times. A genuine friend stands by us through good times and challenges, offering encouragement and strength. These relationships enrich our lives, providing emotional and spiritual support. Valuing true friendships involves investing time and effort, being present, and showing love and care. By nurturing these connections, we build lasting bonds that reflect God's love and faithfulness.

Prayer:

Lord, help me to recognize the value of true friendship. Teach me to be a loyal and loving friend, reflecting Your faithfulness in my relationships. Amen.

JUNE 23

New Friendships

Bible Verse:

"Do not forget to show hospitality to strangers, for by so doing some people have shown hospitality to angels without knowing it." — Hebrews 13:2 (MSG)

Commentary:

Cultivating new friendships is an essential part of building a supportive and enriching social network. Hebrews 13:2 encourages us to show hospitality to strangers, reminding us of the potential blessings that come from welcoming new people into our lives. Forming new friendships involves being receptive, approachable, and genuinely interested in others. By reaching out and offering kindness, we create opportunities for meaningful connections. Cultivating new friendships adds diversity and richness to our social circles, enhancing our lives with fresh perspectives and experiences.

Prayer:

Heavenly Father, help me to cultivate new friendships with an open heart. Teach me to be welcoming and kind, creating opportunities for meaningful connections that reflect Your love. Amen.

JUNE 24

Supporting Friends Through Difficult Times

Bible Verse:

"Carry each other's burdens, and in this way, you will fulfill the law of Christ."— Galatians 6:2 (MSG)

Commentary:

Supporting friends through difficult times is a vital aspect of friendship. Galatians 6:2 calls us to carry each other's burdens, fulfilling the law of Christ through acts of love and compassion. Being there for a friend during tough times involves listening, offering practical help, and providing emotional support. By sharing their struggles, we demonstrate empathy and strengthen the bond of friendship. Supporting and uplifting friends in need not only comforts them but also deepens our connection, reflecting the selfless love of Christ.

Prayer:

Lord, help me to support my friends through difficult times. Teach me to carry their burdens with love and compassion, fulfilling Your command to love one another. Amen.

JUNE 25

Navigating Friendships in Adulthood

Bible Verse:

"Two are better than one because they have a good return for their labor: If either of them falls down, one can help the other up."— Ecclesiastes 4:9-10 (MSG)

Commentary:

Navigating friendships in adulthood requires intentional effort and adaptability. Ecclesiastes 4:9-10 reminds us of the importance of companionship, emphasizing the benefits of mutual support. As life changes, maintaining friendships can become challenging due to busy schedules and evolving priorities. However, by prioritizing connections and making time for friends, we can sustain lasting relationships. Adult friendships provide support, encouragement, and shared experiences, enriching our lives and helping us navigate life's ups and downs with grace.

Prayer:

Heavenly Father, help me navigate adulthood friendships with wisdom and grace. Teach me to prioritize connection and support, building lasting relationships that honor You. Amen.

The Role of Vulnerability in Friendship

Bible Verse:

"Therefore, confess your sins to each other and pray for each other so that you may be healed." — James 5:16 (MSG)

Commentary:

Vulnerability plays a crucial role in deepening friendships. James 5:16 encourages us to confess our sins to one another and pray for each other, fostering transparency and trust. Being vulnerable means sharing our true selves, including our struggles, fears, and failures. This openness creates a safe space for mutual support and understanding. When we are vulnerable with friends, we build deeper connections, promote healing, and strengthen the bonds of friendship, reflecting the grace and love of Christ.

Prayer:

Lord, teach me to embrace vulnerability in my friendships. Help me to share openly and honestly, building deeper connections based on trust and mutual support. Amen.

JUNE 27

Finding Community and Belonging

Bible Verse:

"For where two or three gather in my name, there am I with them." — Matthew 18:20 (MSG)

Commentary:

Finding community and belonging is essential for emotional and spiritual well-being. Matthew 18:20 assures us of God's presence when we gather together in His name, highlighting the importance of community. Being part of a supportive group provides a sense of belonging, encouragement, and accountability. Community helps us grow in faith, share our joys and struggles, and build lasting friendships. By seeking out and engaging in communities that align with our values and principles, we create a network of support that nurtures our growth and enriches our lives.

Prayer:

Heavenly Father, help me to find and nurture a sense of community and belonging. Teach me to engage with others in meaningful ways, building connections that reflect Your love and support. Amen.

JUNE 28

Balancing Time Between Friends and Family

Bible Verse:

"Let us not become weary in doing good, for at the proper time we will reap a harvest if we do not give up." — Galatians 6:9 (MSG)

Commentary:

Balancing time between friends and family is crucial for maintaining healthy relationships. Galatians 6:9 encourages us not to grow weary in doing good, reminding us of the rewards of perseverance and balance. Managing time wisely ensures that we nurture both friendships and family bonds, allowing each to flourish. Prioritizing quality time with loved ones and setting healthy boundaries helps maintain strong, supportive relationships. By balancing our commitments, we create a harmonious life that honors our relationships and reflects God's love.

Prayer:

Lord, help me to balance my time between friends and family. Teach me to manage my commitments wisely, nurturing both friendships and family bonds in a way that honors You. Amen.

JUNE 29

Serving Others in Your Relationships

Bible Verse:

"For even the Son of Man did not come to be served, but to serve, and to give his life as a ransom for many." — Mark 10:45 (MSG)

Commentary:

Serving others in our relationships is a reflection of Christ's example of love and humility. Mark 10:45 reminds us that Jesus came to serve, not to be served, and gave His life for others. In our relationships, we are called to serve with a selfless heart, putting the needs of others before our own. By doing so, we demonstrate God's love and create deeper, enriched connections. Serving others fosters a spirit of generosity and compassion, building strong relationships based on love and mutual respect.

Prayer:

Lord, help me to serve others in my relationships. Teach me to follow Christ's example of selfless love and humility, building connections that reflect Your grace. Amen.

Finding God in Your Relationships

Bible Verse:

"As iron sharpens iron, so one person sharpens another." — Proverbs 27:17 (MSG)

Commentary:

Finding God in our relationships involves recognizing His presence and influence in our interactions with others. Proverbs 27:17 illustrates how relationships can help us grow and improve, just as iron sharpens iron. When we see our relationships as opportunities to learn, grow, and encourage one another, we can appreciate God's work. By seeking His guidance and wisdom, we can foster connections that honor Him and contribute to our spiritual growth. Seeing God in our relationships helps us appreciate the blessings of companionship and encourages us to love others as He loves us.

Prayer:

Heavenly Father, help me to find You in my relationships. Teach me to see Your hand at work in my interactions with others and to foster connections that honor and reflect Your love. Amen.

WELCOME TO THE MONTH OF JULY –
THEME: CREATIVITY AND SELF-EXPRESSION

JULY 1

Unlocking Your Creative Spirit

Bible Verse:

"For we are God's handiwork, created in Christ Jesus to do good works, which God prepared in advance for us to do." — Ephesians 2:10 (MSG)

Commentary:

Unlocking your creative spirit begins with recognizing that you are a unique creation of God, designed with purpose and potential. Ephesians 2:10 reminds us that we are God's handiwork, crafted to do good works that He has prepared for us. Embracing your creativity is an act of honoring the Creator who fashioned you. By exploring your creative gifts, you tap into the divine spark within you, allowing you to express yourself and glorify God through your unique talents and abilities.

Prayer:

Heavenly Father, help me unlock my creative spirit. Teach me to recognize and use the gifts You have given me to glorify You and serve others. Amen.

JULY 2

The Power of Imagination

Bible Verse:

"Now to him who is able to do immeasurably more than all we ask or imagine, according to his power that is at work within us." — Ephesians 3:20 (MSG)

Commentary:

The power of imagination is a beautiful gift from God that allows us to dream and envision possibilities beyond our current reality. Ephesians 3:20 speaks to God's ability to do more than we can ask or imagine, emphasizing the limitless potential of our imagination when aligned with God's power. By cultivating your imagination, you open yourself to creative inspiration and innovative thinking. Imagination fuels creativity, helping you explore new ideas and express yourself in ways that reflect God's infinite creativity.

Prayer:

Lord, inspire my imagination to dream big and to see the endless possibilities with You. Help me use my imagination to create and to bring glory to Your name. Amen.

JULY 3

Embracing Artistic Expression

Bible Verse:

"Sing to the Lord a new song; sing to the Lord, all the earth." — Psalm 96:1 (MSG)

Commentary:

Embracing artistic expression is an invitation to worship God through creativity. Psalm 96:1 calls us to sing a new song to the Lord, encouraging us to use our artistic talents to praise and glorify God. Whether through music, painting, writing, or any other form of art, artistic expression of ourselves allows us to connect with God on a deeper level. Artistic expression is a form of worship that reflects God's creativity and celebrates His beauty, love, and majesty in a unique and personal way.

Prayer:

Heavenly Father, help me embrace artistic expression as a way to worship You. Teach me to use my creative gifts to praise You and to reflect Your glory. Amen.

JULY 4

Finding Inspiration in Nature

Bible Verse:

"The heavens declare the glory of God; the skies proclaim the work of his hands." — Psalm 19:1 (MSG)

Commentary:

Finding inspiration in nature allows us to connect with God's creation and recognize His hand in the world around us. Psalm 19:1 beautifully describes how the heavens and skies proclaim God's glory, reminding us that nature is a testament to His creativity and power. By observing the beauty of the natural world, we can find endless sources of inspiration for our creative endeavors. Nature's diversity, colors, and patterns inspire us to see God's artistry and to express our appreciation and wonder for His creation through our creative work.

Prayer:

Lord, open my eyes to see Your beauty in nature. Inspire me through Your creation to express my creativity in ways that honor You and reflect Your glory. Amen.

JULY 5

Breaking Free from Creative Blocks

Bible Verse:

"I can do all this through him who gives me strength." — Philippians 4:13 (MSG)

Commentary:

Breaking free from creative blocks requires reliance on God's strength and guidance. Seeking God to guide our instincts and creativity can be one way to tackle creative emancipation. Philippians 4:13 reminds us that we can do all things through Christ who strengthens us, including overcoming obstacles that hinder our creativity. Creative blocks can be frustrating, but by turning to God for inspiration and perseverance, we can find new ways to move forward. Trusting in God's strength allows us to push past barriers and tap into the creativity He has placed within us, enabling us to create with renewed passion and purpose.

Prayer:

Heavenly Father, help me to break free from any creative blocks I face. Strengthen me and guide me so I can create with passion and purpose, glorifying You in all I do. Amen.

JULY 6

The Joy of Creating

Bible Verse:

"The Lord your God is with you, the Mighty Warrior who saves. He will take great delight in you; in his love, he will no longer rebuke you but will rejoice over you with singing." — Zephaniah 3:17 (MSG)

Commentary:

The joy of creating is a reflection of the delight God takes in us. Zephaniah 3:17 describes how God rejoices over us with singing, illustrating His deep love and joy in His creation. When we engage in creative activities, we mirror God's joy in creating. The process of creating draws us closer to God, allowing us to experience a sense of fulfillment and happiness. By embracing the joy of creating, we celebrate God's creativity and express our gratitude for the gifts He has given us.

Prayer:

Lord, help me find joy in creating and to see it as a way to connect with You. Teach me to delight in the creative process, knowing that You rejoice over me with love and singing. Amen.

JULY 7

Creativity as a Gift from God

Bible Verse:

"We have different gifts, according to the grace given to each of us." — Romans 12:6 (MSG)

Commentary:

Creativity is a unique gift from God, bestowed upon us by His grace. Romans 12:6 reminds us that we all have different gifts, and creativity is one of the many ways God expresses His grace through us. Recognizing creativity as a divine gift allows us to use it purposefully to honor God and bless others. By embracing our creative talents, we become stewards of the gifts God has given us, using them to contribute to His kingdom and to reflect His love and beauty in the world.

Prayer:

Heavenly Father, thank You for the gift of creativity. Help me to use this gift to honor You and to bless others, reflecting Your grace and love in all I create. Amen.

JULY 8

Developing a Creative Routine

Bible Verse:

"But seek first his kingdom and his righteousness, and all these things will be given to you as well." — Matthew 6:33 (MSG)

Commentary:

Developing a creative routine involves prioritizing time for creativity just as we prioritize our spiritual lives. Matthew 6:33 encourages us to seek God first, trusting that everything else will fall into place. Similarly, when we establish a routine that includes dedicated time for creative activities, we allow space for inspiration to flow. Regular creative practice helps us stay focused, nurtures our talents, and allows us to use our gifts for God's magnificence. By being intentional about our creative routines, we honor the gifts God has given us and cultivate a mindset of growth and creativity.

Prayer:

Lord, help me to develop a routine that prioritizes creativity and honors You. Teach me to seek Your guidance in all I do, making time for the creative gifts You have given me. Amen.

JULY 9

Seeing the World with Fresh Eyes

Bible Verse:

"Open my eyes that I may see wonderful things in your law." — Psalm 119:18 (MSG)

Commentary:

Seeing the world with fresh eyes means approaching each DAY with a sense of wonder and curiosity. Psalm 119:18 is a prayer asking God to open our eyes to the beauty and wisdom of His Word. Similarly, we can ask God to open our eyes to the wonders of the world around us. By viewing our surroundings with a fresh perspective, we become more attuned to the details, colors, and patterns that can inspire our creativity. This practice encourages us to appreciate everyday moments and see them as opportunities for creative expression.

Prayer:

Heavenly Father, open my eyes to see the world with fresh eyes. Help me find inspiration every day and use what I see to express my creativity in ways that honor You. Amen.

JULY 10

Embracing Curiosity

Bible Verse:

"Ask, and it will be given to you; seek and you will find; knock and the door will be opened to you." — Matthew 7:7 (MSG)

Commentary:

Embracing curiosity is a vital part of cultivating a creative mindset. Matthew 7:7 encourages us to ask, seek, and knock, highlighting the importance of curiosity in our spiritual journey. Curiosity leads us to explore new ideas, ask questions, and seek knowledge. By maintaining a inquisitive mindset, we open ourselves up to new experiences and creative possibilities. Embracing curiosity allows us to see the world from different perspectives, fueling our creativity and leading to innovative ideas.

Prayer:

Lord, help me to embrace curiosity and seek new ideas. Teach me to be open to new experiences and to use my curiosity to fuel my creativity, always seeking Your wisdom. Amen.

JULY 11

The Role of Play in Creativity

Bible Verse:

"A joyful heart is good medicine, but a crushed spirit dries up the bones." — Proverbs 17:22 (MSG)

Commentary:

The role of play in creativity is essential for maintaining a joyful and inventive spirit. Proverbs 17:22 reminds us that a joyful heart is good medicine, emphasizing the importance of joy in our lives. Playfulness brings lightness and fun to the creative process, allowing us to experiment without fear of failure. Engaging in playful activities stimulates the mind and encourages spontaneous and innovative thinking. By incorporating play into our creative practices, we foster a sense of joy and liberty that enhances our ability to create.

Prayer:

Heavenly Father, help me to embrace the role of play in my creativity. Teach me to approach my creative work with a joyful heart and a spirit of playfulness, reflecting Your joy and love. Amen.

Overcoming Fear of Judgment

Bible Verse:

"The fear of man lays a snare, but whoever trusts in the Lord is safe." — Proverbs 29:25 (MSG)

Commentary:

Overcoming the fear of judgment is crucial for authentic self-expression. Proverbs 29:25 teaches that fearing others can be a trap, but trusting in the Lord brings safety. Fear of judgment can stifle our creativity and prevent us from expressing our true selves. By placing our trust in God and seeking His approval rather than the approval of others, we can find the courage to create freely. Embracing our creativity without fear allows us to express our unique gifts and talents, honoring God with our authentic selves.

Prayer:

Lord, help me to overcome the fear of judgment and to trust in You. Teach me to express my creativity boldly and authentically, knowing that my worth is found in You alone. Amen.

JULY 13

Exploring Different Mediums

Bible Verse:

"There are different kinds of gifts, but the same Spirit distributes them." — 1 Corinthians 12:4 (MSG)

Commentary:

Exploring different creative mediums allows us to discover new ways of expressing ourselves. 1 Corinthians 12:4 reminds us that there are various gifts, all given by the same Spirit. Just as there are different spiritual gifts, there are also different ways to be creative and imaginative. By trying out various mediums—whether it be painting, writing, music, or sculpture—we can find new avenues for self-expression. This exploration helps us expand our creative horizons and appreciate the diversity of gifts that God has given us.

Prayer:

Heavenly Father, help me to explore different creative mediums. Teach me to use my diverse talents to express myself and to honor You with the gifts You have given me. Amen.

Creativity in Problem Solving

Bible Verse:

"If any of you lacks wisdom, you should ask God, who gives generously to all without finding fault, and it will be given to you." — James 1:5 (MSG)

Commentary:

Creativity in problem-solving is a valuable skill that enables us to approach challenges with fresh perspectives. James 1:5 encourages us to seek wisdom from God, who generously provides it. Creativity allows us to think outside the box and find innovative solutions to the problems we face. By applying creative thinking to our everyday challenges, we can discover new ways to overcome obstacles, improve our circumstances, and help us grow. Embracing creativity in problem-solving helps us grow in wisdom and trust in God's guidance.

Prayer:

Lord, grant me creativity in problem-solving and the wisdom to seek Your guidance. Teach me to approach challenges with a creative mindset and to find innovative solutions that honor You. Amen.

JULY 15

Writing as a Form of Self-Expression

Bible Verse:

"May these words of my mouth and this meditation of my heart be pleasing in your sight, Lord, my Rock and my Redeemer." — Psalm 19:14 (MSG)

Commentary:

Writing is a powerful tool for expressing thoughts, emotions, and faith. Psalm 19:14 reflects the desire for our words and meditations to be pleasing to God, highlighting the importance of intentional expression. Through writing, we can explore our inner world, document our spiritual journey, and share our experiences with others. Writing allows us to communicate our deepest feelings, celebrate our joys, and process our entangled thoughts. By using writing as a form of self-expression, we honor God with our words and offer encouragement and inspiration to those around us.

Prayer:

Lord, help me to use writing as a way to express myself and honor You. Teach me to communicate my thoughts and feelings with authenticity, sharing my journey in a way that pleases You. Amen.

The Art of Storytelling

Bible Verse:

"Jesus spoke all these things to the crowd in parables; he did not say anything to them without using a parable." — Matthew 13:34 (MSG)

Commentary:

Storytelling is a compelling way to convey truth, wisdom, and experiences. Matthew 13:34 shows that Jesus often used parables to teach, illustrating the power of stories in imparting spiritual lessons. Storytelling allows us to connect with others on a deep emotional level, sharing our experiences and insights in a relatable and engaging way. By telling our stories, we can motivate, uplift, and teach others, using our personal narratives to communicate God's love and grace.

Prayer:

Heavenly Father, teach me the art of storytelling. Help me to share my experiences and lessons learned in a way that inspires and encourages others, reflecting Your truth and love. Amen.

JULY 17

Music as a Means of Worship

Bible Verse:

"Sing and make music from your heart to the Lord."
— Ephesians 5:19 (MSG)

Commentary:

Music is a beautiful means of worship and a powerful form of self-expression. Ephesians 5:19 encourages us to make music from our hearts to the Lord, highlighting the role of music in praising God. Through music, we can express our love, gratitude, and devotion to God in a unique and impactful way. Whether singing, playing an instrument, or composing, music allows us to connect with God and others on a deep spiritual level. By using music as a means of worship, we honor God with our ingenuity and share His love through our melodies.

Prayer:

Lord, help me to use music as a means of worship and self-expression. Teach me to make music from my heart that glorifies You and draws others closer to Your presence. Amen.

Visual Art and Spiritual Reflection

Bible Verse:

"He has filled them with skill to do all kinds of work as engravers, designers, embroiderers in blue, purple and scarlet yarn and fine linen, and weavers—all of them skilled workers and designers." — Exodus 35:35 (MSG)

Commentary:

Visual art is a powerful medium for spiritual reflection and expression. Exodus 35:35 describes how God endowed certain individuals with artistic skills, emphasizing the value of creativity in worship and spiritual life. Through visual art, we can explore our faith, express our sentiments, and reflect on God's character and works. Painting, drawing, and other forms of visual art allow us to meditate on spiritual themes and communicate our inner experiences visually. By engaging in visual art, we can deepen our connection with God and share our spiritual journey with others.

Prayer:

Heavenly Father, help me to use visual art as a tool for spiritual reflection and expression. Teach me to create works that honor You and reflect my faith journey, sharing Your love and beauty with the world. Amen.

JULY 19

Dance as an Expression of Joy

Bible Verse:

"Let them praise his name with dancing and make music to him with timbrel and harp." — Psalm 149:3 (MSG)

Commentary:

Dance is a vibrant form of self-expression that can be used to express joy, praise, and gratitude. Psalm 149:3 encourages us to praise God with dancing, illustrating the joy and celebration that dance can convey. Through dance, we can express our emotions, release our inhibitions, and connect with God dynamically and physically. Dance allows us to celebrate the freedom and joy we have in Christ, using our bodies to glorify God. By embracing dance as a form of expression, we can experience a deeper sense of joy and connection with God.

Prayer:

Lord, help me to use dance as a form of expression and worship. Teach me to celebrate Your love and grace through movement, using my body to glorify You with joy and freedom. Amen.

Crafting with Purpose

Bible Verse:

"She selects wool and flax and works with eager hands." — Proverbs 31:13 (MSG)

Commentary:

Crafting with purpose involves using our creativity to make meaningful and beautiful objects that reflect our values and faith. Proverbs 31:13 describes a woman who works with eager hands, highlighting the joy and purpose found in creative work. Crafting can be a mindful practice that allows us to express ourselves, relax, and create items that serve a purpose. Whether knitting, woodworking, or making jewelry, crafting with intention allows us to use our hands to create something meaningful. By crafting with purpose, we honor God with our creativity and share our gifts with others.

Prayer:

Heavenly Father, help me to craft with purpose and intention. Teach me to use my creativity to create beautiful and meaningful items that reflect my faith and bless others. Amen.

Photography and the Art of Seeing

Bible Verse:

"The eye is the lamp of the body. If your eyes are healthy, your whole body will be full of light." — Matthew 6:22 (MSG)

Commentary:

Photography is an art form that captures the beauty of God's creation and invites us to see the world through a different lens. Matthew 6:22 speaks of the eye as the lamp of the body, emphasizing the importance of seeing clearly and with purpose. Photography allows us to pause, observe, and appreciate the intricate details of our surroundings, capturing moments that reflect God's handiwork. By using photography as a form of self-expression, we can share our unique perspective and highlight the beauty of God's world.

Prayer:

Lord, help me to use photography as a way to see the world through Your eyes. Teach me to capture the beauty of Your creation and to share it with others, reflecting Your glory. Amen.

JULY 22

Creating a Sacred Space for Creativity

Bible Verse:

"But when you pray, go into your room, close the door, and pray to your Father, who is unseen. Then your Father, who sees what is done in secret, will reward you." — Matthew 6:6 (MSG)

Commentary:

Creating a sacred space for creativity allows us to focus our minds and hearts on the act of creating, much like a prayer closet allows for focused communication with God. Matthew 6:6 encourages us to find a quiet place for prayer, suggesting the importance of setting aside a dedicated space for spiritual and creative practices. A sacred creative space can be a room, a corner, or even a desk where we feel inspired and free to express ourselves. By dedicating a space to creativity, we invite God's presence into our creative process and nurture our artistic gifts.

Prayer:

Heavenly Father, help me to create a sacred space for creativity. Teach me to use this space to connect with You and to express my creativity in ways that honor You. Amen.

Finding Beauty in the Ordinary

Bible Verse:

"He has made everything beautiful in its time." — Ecclesiastes 3:11 (MSG)

Commentary:

Finding beauty in the ordinary involves recognizing the divine in everyday moments. Ecclesiastes 3:11 reminds us that God has made everything beautiful in its time, highlighting the inherent beauty in all of creation. By paying attention to the small, seemingly mundane details of life, we can find inspiration and see God's handiwork. This practice prompts us to appreciate the simple things and to express our creativity through the lens of gratitude and wonder. Seeing beauty in the ordinary enriches our creative expression and deepens our connection to God's creation.

Prayer:

Lord, help me to find beauty in the ordinary moments of life. Teach me to appreciate the simple things and to see Your hand in all things, inspiring my creativity. Amen.

JULY 24

Journaling for Creative Clarity

Bible Verse:

"Write down the revelation and make it plain on tablets so that a herald may run with it." — Habakkuk 2:2 (MSG)

Commentary:

Journaling is a powerful tool for gaining creative clarity and capturing inspiration. Habakkuk 2:2 emphasizes the importance of writing down revelations, making them clear and accessible. Journaling allows us to document our thoughts, ideas, and reflections, providing a space for introspection and creative exploration. By regularly journaling, we can clarify our creative vision, track our progress, and reflect on our growth. This practice helps us stay focused and inspired, nurturing our imagination and allowing us to creatively convey ourselves better.

Prayer:

Heavenly Father, help me to use journaling as a tool for creative clarity. Teach me to capture my thoughts and inspirations on paper, guiding me in my creative journey. Amen.

JULY 25

Collaborating with Others

Bible Verse:

"Two are better than one because they have a good return for their labor." — Ecclesiastes 4:9 (MSG)

Commentary:

Collaborating with others can enhance creativity and lead to new ideas and perspectives. Ecclesiastes 4:9 highlights the benefits of working together, emphasizing the strength and productivity that comes from collaboration. By partnering with others, we can combine our unique talents and skills, fostering a spirit of teamwork and mutual support. Collaboration allows us to learn from one another, share inspiration, and create something greater than we could on our own. Working with others enriches our creative process and builds meaningful connections.

Prayer:

Lord, help me to embrace collaboration in my creative endeavors. Teach me to work with others, sharing my gifts and learning from theirs, creating beautiful things together. Amen.

JULY 26

Gratitude for Your Creative Gifts

Bible Verse:

"Give thanks to the Lord, for he is good; his love endures forever." — Psalm 107:1 (MSG)

Commentary:

Practicing gratitude for your creative gifts is essential for nurturing a positive and productive creative mindset. Psalm 107:1 encourages us to give thanks to the Lord for His goodness and enduring love. By expressing gratitude for the creative talents God has given us, we acknowledge His grace and generosity. Gratitude shifts our focus from what we lack to what we have, fostering a sense of contentment and joy. Practicing gratitude for our creative abilities helps us to use them purposefully, honoring God and blessing others with our talents.

Prayer:

Heavenly Father, help me to practice gratitude for my creative gifts. Teach me to appreciate the talents You have given me and to use them to glorify You and bless others. Amen.

Connection Between Creativity and Spirituality

Bible Verse:

"In the beginning, God created the heavens and the earth." — Genesis 1:1 (MSG)

Commentary:

Exploring the connection between creativity and spirituality reveals the divine nature of our creative instincts. Genesis 1:1 begins with God as the Creator, establishing the foundation of creativity as a divine attribute. As beings made in God's image, our creativity reflects His creative nature. Engaging in creative activities can be a spiritual practice that draws us closer to God, allowing us to express our faith, explore our inner selves, and communicate God's love and beauty. By understanding creativity as a spiritual practice, we can use our talents to glorify God and grow in our relationship with Him.

Prayer:

Lord, help me to explore the connection between creativity and spirituality. Teach me to use my creativity as a way to connect with You and to express my faith in meaningful ways. Amen.

JULY 28

Celebrating Your Creative Achievements

Bible Verse:

"The Lord has done great things for us, and we are filled with joy." — Psalm 126:3 (MSG)

Commentary:

Celebrating your creative achievements is an important part of honoring the gifts God has given you. Psalm 126:3 reflects on the great things the Lord has done, encouraging us to recognize and rejoice in His blessings. Acknowledging your creative successes, no matter how small, helps you value the progress you have made and the talents you possess. Celebrating your achievements fosters a positive mindset, motivates you to continue creating, and reinforces the value of your creative contributions. By taking time to celebrate, you honor God and express gratitude for His gifts.

Prayer:

Heavenly Father, help me to celebrate my creative achievements with gratitude. Teach me to recognize the progress I have made and to give You the glory for the gifts You have given me. Amen.

Using Your Creativity to Serve Others

Bible Verse:

"Each of you should use whatever gift you have received to serve others as faithful stewards of God's grace in its various forms." — 1 Peter 4:10 (MSG)

Commentary:

Using your creativity to serve others is a powerful way to share God's love and grace. 1 Peter 4:10 encourages us to use our gifts to serve others, reminding us that our talents are entrusted to us for a purpose. By applying our creative abilities in service to others, we become stewards of God's grace, reflecting His love through our actions, whether through art, music, writing, or other creative pursuits. Sharing our talents to uplift others brings them joy and honors God.

Prayer:

Lord, help me to use my creativity to serve others. Teach me to be a faithful steward of the gifts You have given me, using them to share Your love and grace with those around me. Amen.

Finding Your Unique Creative Voice

Bible Verse:

"For you created my inmost being; you knit me together in my mother's womb." — Psalm 139:13 (MSG)

Commentary:

Finding your unique creative voice is about discovering how your individuality can express the divine. Psalm 139:13 reminds us that God created each of us with care and intention, emphasizing our uniqueness. Your creative voice is a reflection of who you are—your experiences, perspectives, and emotions. By exploring different forms of expression and staying true to yourself, you can find a creative style that is authentically yours. Embracing your unique creative voice allows you to honor God with your individuality and share your personal story with the world.

Prayer:

Heavenly Father, help me to find my unique creative voice. Teach me to express myself authentically, reflecting Your design and purpose for my life. Amen.

JULY 31

Committing to a Life of Creative Exploration

Bible Verse:

"But as for you, be strong and do not give up, for your work will be rewarded."— 2 Chronicles 15:7 (MSG)

Commentary:

Committing to a life of creative exploration means embracing creativity as an ongoing journey. 2 Chronicles 15:7 encourages us to be strong and not give up, promising that our efforts will be rewarded. A creative life involves persistently seeking new ideas, learning new skills, and experimenting with different forms of expression. By committing to this exploration, we keep our creative spirit alive and open to God's leading. A life of creative exploration is a life of growth, discovery, and fulfillment as we use our gifts to honor God and serve others.

Prayer:

Lord, help me to commit to a life of creative exploration. Teach me to be strong and perseverant in my creative journey, using my gifts to glorify You and bring joy to others. Amen.

WELCOME TO THE MONTH OF AUGUST –
THEME: MINDFULNESS AND PRESENT LIVING

AUGUST 1

The Essence of Mindfulness

Bible Verse:

"Be still, and know that I am God." — Psalm 46:10 (MSG)

Commentary:

The essence of mindfulness is about being fully present in each moment and aware of God's presence in our lives. Psalm 46:10 invites us to be still and acknowledge God, emphasizing the importance of pausing to experience His presence. Mindfulness involves quieting our minds and focusing our thoughts on the here and now, allowing us to connect more deeply with God and ourselves. By practicing mindfulness, we become more attuned to our inner lives and more aware of God's work around us, fostering a deeper sense of peace and connection.

Prayer:

Lord, help me to understand the essence of mindfulness and to be fully present in each moment. Teach me to be still and to recognize Your presence in my life. Amen.

AUGUST 2

Living in the Present Moment

Bible Verse:

"Therefore, do not worry about tomorrow, for tomorrow will worry about itself. Each DAY has enough trouble of its own." — Matthew 6:34 (MSG)

Commentary:

Living in the present moment means focusing on today rather than worrying about the future. Matthew 6:34 encourages us to avoid anxiety about tomorrow, emphasizing that each DAY has its own concerns. By concentrating on the present, we free ourselves from unnecessary worries that might hinder us from cultivating peaceful midnset and fully engage with the people and experiences around us. Mindfulness helps us appreciate the beauty of each moment and deepens our trust in God's provision for our lives. Living in the present allows us to experience God's peace and guidance more fully.

Prayer:

Heavenly Father, teach me to live in the present moment and to trust in Your care for my future. Help me to focus on today and to find peace in Your presence. Amen.

AUGUST 3

Mindful Breathing

Bible Verse:

"The breath of the Almighty gives me life." — Job 33:4 (MSG)

Commentary:

Mindful breathing is a practice that helps us center our thoughts and connect with God's life-giving presence. Job 33:4 acknowledges that the breath of God gives us life, reminding us of the divine gift of every breath we take. By focusing on our breath, we can calm our minds and bring ourselves into the present moment. This simple yet powerful practice allows us to release tension, quiet distractions, and draw closer to God. Mindful breathing helps us find peace and clarity, grounding us in God's love and grace.

Prayer:

Lord, help me to practice mindful breathing and to find peace in each breath. Teach me to use this practice to center my thoughts and to connect with Your life-giving presence. Amen.

Awareness of Your Surroundings

Bible Verse:

"The earth is the Lord's, and everything in it, the world, and all who live in it." — Psalm 24:1 (MSG)

Commentary:

Being aware of your surroundings involves identifying the beauty and wonder of God's creation in everyday life. Psalm 24:1 reminds us that the earth and everything in it belong to the Lord, encouraging us to appreciate the world around us. By paying attention to our environment, we can see God's hand in the details of creation—the colors of a sunset, the sound of birds singing, or the feel of the breeze. This mindfulness practice helps us connect with God through nature, fostering gratitude and awe for His creation.

Prayer:

Heavenly Father, open my eyes to be aware of my surroundings and to appreciate the beauty of Your creation. Help me to see Your hand in everything around me and to give thanks for Your wondrous works. Amen.

AUGUST 5

Mindfulness and Gratitude

Bible Verse:

"Give thanks in all circumstances, for this is God's will for you in Christ Jesus." — 1 Thessalonians 5:18 (MSG)

Commentary:

Mindfulness and gratitude go hand in hand, helping us cultivate a thankful heart in all circumstances. 1 Thessalonians 5:18 encourages us to give thanks in every situation, recognizing that gratitude is God's will for us. By being mindful of our blessings, we become more aware of the good in our lives, even amid life's up and down. Practicing gratitude helps us shift our focus from what we lack to what we have, fostering a positive outlook and deepening our appreciation for God's provision.

Prayer:

Lord, help me to be mindful of the blessings in my life and to cultivate a heart of gratitude. Teach me to give thanks in all circumstances, recognizing Your goodness and grace. Amen.

AUGUST 6

Overcoming Distractions

Bible Verse:

"Set your minds on things above, not on earthly things." — Colossians 3:2 (MSG)

Commentary:

Overcoming distractions is essential for practicing mindfulness and staying focused on what truly matters. Colossians 3:2 urges us to set our minds on things above, not on earthly distractions. In our busy world, it's easy to become overwhelmed by noise and activity, losing sight of God's presence and purpose. By practicing mindfulness, we can learn to let go of distractions and refocus our thoughts on God and His kingdom. Overcoming distractions helps us stay present and centered, fostering a deeper connection with God and a more intentional approach to life.

Prayer:

Heavenly Father, help me to overcome distractions and to set my mind on things above. Teach me to stay focused on You and to live each moment with intention and purpose. Amen.

AUGUST 7

Mindful Eating

Bible Verse:

"So whether you eat or drink or whatever you do, do it all for the glory of God." — 1 Corinthians 10:31 (MSG)

Commentary:

Mindful eating is the practice of being fully present while eating, appreciating the nourishment God provides. 1 Corinthians 10:31 reminds us to do everything for God's glory, including eating and drinking. By paying attention to the taste, texture, and aroma of our food, we can savor each bite and express gratefulness for God's provision. Mindful eating helps us develop a healthier relationship with food and our bodies, fostering a sense of gratitude and stewardship for the resources God has given us.

Prayer:

Lord, help me to practice mindful eating and to appreciate the nourishment You provide. Teach me to eat with gratitude and intention, honoring You in all I do. Amen.

Mindfulness in Daily Routines

Bible Verse:

"Whatever you do, work at it with all your heart, as working for the Lord, not for human masters." — Colossians 3:23 (MSG)

Commentary:

Incorporating mindfulness into daily routines transforms ordinary tasks into acts of worship. Colossians 3:23 encourages us to work with all our hearts as if working for the Lord. By being fully present in each task, whether it's washing dishes, commuting to work, or folding laundry, we honor God in the mundane. Mindfulness in daily routines helps us find joy in simplicity, reduces stress, and enhances our appreciation for the moment. This practice turns every activity into a chance to connect with God and live a purposeful life.

Prayer:

Lord, help me to be mindful in my daily routines. Teach me to approach each task with a heart full of gratitude and to see my work as an offering to You. Amen.

AUGUST 9

Mindful Walking

Bible Verse:

"He has shown you, O mortal, what is good. And what does the Lord require of you? To act justly and to love mercy and to walk humbly with your God."—Micah 6:8 (MSG)

Commentary:

Mindful walking is a practice that summons us to be fully present in our steps, experiencing God's presence with every stride. Micah 6:8 calls us to walk humbly with God, suggesting a deliberate, attentive approach to our journey. By paying attention to each step, feeling the ground beneath us, and noticing our surroundings, we can connect more deeply with our bodies and the world around us. Mindful walking helps us slow down, reduces anxiety, and fosters a deeper sense of peace and connection with God.

Prayer:

Heavenly Father, help me to practice mindful walking and to walk humbly with You. Teach me to be aware of each step and to experience Your presence in my journey. Amen.

AUGUST 10

Mindfulness at Work

Bible Verse:

"Commit to the Lord whatever you do, and he will establish your plans." — Proverbs 16:3 (MSG)

Commentary:

Mindfulness at work involves dedicating our professional tasks to God and focusing on His presence throughout the DAY. Proverbs 16:3 encourages us to commit our work to the Lord, trusting that He will guide us. By staying present and fully engaged in our work, we can perform our tasks with excellence and integrity. Mindfulness at work reduces stress, increases productivity, and enhances job satisfaction. It also helps us see our work as a form of worship, honoring God through our efforts.

Prayer:

Lord, help me to practice mindfulness at work and to commit all my tasks to You. Teach me to stay focused, perform with integrity, and see my work as a form of worship. Amen.

AUGUST 11

Mindful Communication

Bible Verse:

"Let your conversation be always full of grace, seasoned with salt, so that you may know how to answer everyone." — Colossians 4:6 (MSG)

Commentary:

Mindful communication involves speaking and listening with intention, grace, and empathy. Colossians 4:6 urges us to ensure our conversations are full of grace, suggesting a mindful approach to how we interact with others. By being fully present in our conversations, we can listen more efficiently, respond thoughtfully, and build stronger relationships. Mindful communication fosters understanding, reduces conflicts, and allows us to express love and respect to those around us. It's an essential practice for cultivating healthy, meaningful connections.

Prayer:

Heavenly Father, help me to practice mindful communication. Teach me to speak with grace, listen with empathy, and honor You in all my interactions with others. Amen.

AUGUST 12

Mindfulness in Prayer

Bible Verse:

"Pray continually." — 1 Thessalonians 5:17 (MSG)

Commentary:

Mindfulness in prayer involves being fully present in our conversations with God, allowing us to connect with Him on a deeper level. 1 Thessalonians 5:17 encourages us to pray continually, suggesting an ongoing, mindful engagement with God. By focusing our thoughts and opening our hearts during prayer, we can experience God's presence more intimately and communicate with Him more authentically. Mindfulness in prayer helps us listen to God's voice, express our needs and gratitude, and grow spiritually within.

Prayer:

Lord, help me to practice mindfulness in prayer. Teach me to be fully present in my time with You, listening for Your voice and sharing my heart with sincerity. Amen.

AUGUST 13

Mindfulness in Relationships

Bible Verse:

"Be devoted to one another in love. Honor one another above yourselves." — Romans 12:10 (MSG)

Commentary:

Mindfulness in relationships involves being fully present with others, showing love, and honoring them above ourselves. Romans 12:10 calls us to be devoted to one another in love, emphasizing the importance of mindful engagement in our relationships. By giving our full attention to those we are with, we show them that they are valued and respected. Mindfulness in relationships enhances communication, builds trust, and fosters profound connections. It allows us to understand others better and to respond with empathy and compassion.

Prayer:

Heavenly Father, help me to practice mindfulness in my relationships. Teach me to be present, to listen attentively, and to honor others with love and respect. Amen.

AUGUST 14

Mindful Rest and Relaxation

Bible Verse:

"Come to me, all you who are weary and burdened, and I will give you rest." — Matthew 11:28 (MSG)

Commentary:

Mindful rest and relaxation are essential for our well-being and spiritual health. Matthew 11:28 invites those who are weary to come to Jesus for rest, highlighting the importance of taking time to recharge. Mindful relaxation involves being fully present in moments of rest, allowing our minds and bodies to unwind and rejuvenate. By intentionally setting aside time for rest and relaxation, we honor the needs of our bodies and create space for God's peace to fill our hearts and souls. This practice helps us maintain balance, reduce stress, and renew our strength.

Prayer:

Lord, help me to practice mindful rest and relaxation. Teach me to set aside time to recharge and to find my rest in You, trusting in Your peace and renewal. Amen.

AUGUST 15

Mindfulness and Stress Management

Bible Verse:

"Cast all your anxiety on him because he cares for you." — 1 Peter 5:7 (MSG)

Commentary:

Mindfulness is a powerful tool for managing stress and finding peace in God's care. 1 Peter 5:7 encourages us to cast all our anxieties on God, knowing that He cares deeply for us. By practicing mindfulness, we become more aware of our stress triggers and can learn to respond calmly rather than react impulsively. Mindfulness helps us stay present, reduce tension, and trust in God's provision and peace. By focusing on the present moment and God's love, we can better manage stress and cultivate a sense of tranquility.

Prayer:

Lord, help me to use mindfulness to manage stress and to trust in Your care. Teach me to cast my anxieties on You and to find peace in Your presence. Amen.

AUGUST 16

Mindful Emotional Awareness

Bible Verse:

"The heart is deceitful above all things and beyond cure. Who can understand it?" — Jeremiah 17:9 (MSG)

Commentary:

Mindful emotional awareness involves recognizing and understanding our emotions without judgment. Jeremiah 17:9 highlights the complexity of the heart, suggesting that our emotions can often be misleading. By practicing mindfulness, we can observe our feelings objectively, allowing ourselves to experience them without being overwhelmed or controlled by them. This awareness helps us wholesomely respond to emotions, fostering emotional balance and well-being. Mindfulness encourages us to bring our emotions to God, seeking His wisdom and guidance in processing them.

Prayer:

Heavenly Father, help me to be mindful of my emotions and to understand them with Your wisdom. Teach me to observe my feelings without judgment and to bring them to You for guidance and healing. Amen.

AUGUST 17

Letting Go of Negative Thoughts

Bible Verse:

"Finally, brothers and sisters, whatever is true, whatever is noble, whatever is right, whatever is pure, whatever is lovely, whatever is admirable—if anything is excellent or praiseworthy—think about such things."— Philippians 4:8 (MSG)

Commentary:

Letting go of negative thoughts is essential for maintaining a positive and healthy mindset. Philippians 4:8 encourages us to focus on what is true, noble, right, pure, lovely, admirable, excellent, and praiseworthy. Mindfulness helps us become aware of negative thought patterns and gently guides us to replace them with thoughts that align with God's truth and goodness. By letting go of negativity, we free ourselves from its weight and open our hearts to joy, peace, and gratitude.

Prayer:

Lord, help me to let go of negative thoughts and to focus on what is good and true. Teach me to align my mind with Your truth and to cultivate a positive, healthy mindset. Amen.

AUGUST 18

Mindfulness and Compassion

Bible Verse:

"Be kind and compassionate to one another, forgiving each other, just as in Christ God forgave you." — Ephesians 4:32 (MSG)

Commentary:

Mindfulness fosters compassion by helping us become more aware of the needs and feelings of others. Ephesians 4:32 calls us to be kind and compassionate, highlighting the importance of empathy in our relationships. By practicing mindfulness, we learn to observe others without judgment and to respond with kindness and understanding. Mindfulness helps us cultivate a compassionate heart, seeing others as God sees them and offering forgiveness and grace. This practice enhances our relationships and echoes God's love to those around us.

Prayer:

Heavenly Father, help me to cultivate mindfulness and compassion in my interactions with others. Teach me to see people as You see them and to respond with kindness, empathy, and grace. Amen.

AUGUST 19

Mindfulness in Forgiveness

Bible Verse:

"Bear with each other and forgive one another if any of you has a grievance against someone. Forgive as the Lord forgave you." — Colossians 3:13 (MSG)

Commentary:

Mindfulness plays a crucial role in the process of forgiveness, helping us let go of bitterness and embrace grace. Colossians 3:13 instructs us to forgive others as the Lord has forgiven us, emphasizing the importance of forgiveness in our spiritual lives. Mindfulness allows us to become aware of our feelings of hurt or anger, acknowledge them, and then release them to God. This practice helps us move beyond grudges and towards healing, fostering a spirit of forgiveness and reconciliation.

Prayer:

Lord, help me to practice mindfulness in forgiveness and to let go of resentment. Teach me to forgive others as You have forgiven me, embracing Your grace and healing. Amen.

AUGUST 20

Embracing Mindful Joy

Bible Verse:

"Rejoice in the Lord always. I will say it again: Rejoice!" — Philippians 4:4 (MSG)

Commentary:

Embracing mindful joy involves being fully present in the moments of happiness and choosing to rejoice in the Lord. Philippians 4:4 calls us to rejoice always, emphasizing the importance of a joyful spirit. Mindfulness helps us savor the moments of joy in our lives, whether big or small, by being fully present and appreciative. This practice augments our overall sense of well-being and draws us closer to God, recognizing His hand in our blessings. Mindful joy allows us to experience life with a heart full of gratitude and praise.

Prayer:

Heavenly Father, help me to embrace mindful joy and to rejoice in You always. Teach me to be fully present in moments of happiness and to recognize Your hand in my blessings. Amen.

AUGUST 21

Mindful Self-Care

Bible Verse:

"Do you not know that your bodies are temples of the Holy Spirit, who is in you, whom you have received from God? You are not your own."— 1 Corinthians 6:19 (MSG)

Commentary:

Mindful self-care is about honoring our bodies as temples of the Holy Spirit and taking intentional steps to care for our well-being. 1 Corinthians 6:19 reminds us that our bodies belong to God and are sacred. Practicing mindfulness in self-care involves listening to our bodies, recognizing their needs, and responding with compassion and care. This includes nourishing ourselves with healthy food, getting adequate rest, exercising, and finding balance in our daily lives. Mindful self-care helps us honor God by tending to the bodies He has given us and nurturing our overall health.

Prayer:

Lord, help me to practice mindful self-care and honor my body as a temple of Your Holy Spirit. Teach me to listen to my body's needs and to care for myself in a way that honors You. Amen.

AUGUST 22

Mindfulness and Spiritual Awareness

Bible Verse:

"You will seek me and find me when you seek me with all your heart." — Jeremiah 29:13 (MSG)

Commentary:

Self-awareness enhances spiritual awareness by helping us focus our hearts and minds on God. Jeremiah 29:13 reminds us that when we seek God with all our hearts, we will find Him. By practicing mindfulness, we become more attuned to God's presence in our daily lives, noticing His guidance, comfort, and love in even the smallest details. Mindfulness encourages us to slow down and pay attention to the ways God is working around us, deepening our spiritual awareness and fostering a closer relationship with Him.

Prayer:

Lord, help me to cultivate mindfulness and deepen my spiritual awareness. Teach me to seek You with all my heart and to recognize Your presence in every moment. Amen.

AUGUST 23

Mindfulness in Scripture Meditation

Bible Verse:

"But his delight is in the law of the Lord, and on his law, he meditates DAY and night." — Psalm 1:2 (MSG)

Commentary:

Mindfulness in Scripture meditation involves focusing intently on God's Word and allowing it to speak to our hearts. Psalm 1:2 encourages us to meditate on God's law DAY and night, highlighting the importance of immersing ourselves in Scripture. By practicing mindfulness while reading the Bible, we can engross ourselves in its wisdom, absorb its teachings more deeply and apply them to our lives. This form of meditation helps us connect with God's truth, find comfort and guidance in His promises, and grow spiritually.

Prayer:

Heavenly Father, help me to practice mindfulness in Scripture meditation. Teach me to focus intently on Your Word and to let it transform my heart and guide my actions. Amen.

AUGUST 24

Mindfulness and Spiritual Discernment

Bible Verse:

"If any of you lacks wisdom, you should ask God, who gives generously to all without finding fault, and it will be given to you." — James 1:5 (MSG)

Commentary:

Mindfulness enhances spiritual discernment by helping us stay attentive to God's voice and guidance. James 1:5 encourages us to seek wisdom from God, who gives generously to all who ask. By practicing mindfulness, we create space in our minds and hearts to hear God's direction and discern His will. This attentiveness allows us to make decisions aligned with God's purpose and to navigate life's challenges with His wisdom. Mindfulness in spiritual discernment helps us trust God more deeply and follow His leading.

Prayer:

Lord, help me to practice mindfulness and seek Your wisdom in all things. Teach me to discern Your will and to follow Your guidance with trust and faith. Amen.

AUGUST 25

Living Mindfully in God's Presence

Bible Verse:

"The Lord your God is with you, the Mighty Warrior who saves. He will take great delight in you; in his love, he will no longer rebuke you but will rejoice over you with singing." — Zephaniah 3:17 (MSG)

Commentary:

Living mindfully in God's presence means being aware of His constant companionship and love. Zephaniah 3:17 reminds us that God is always with us, delighting in us and rejoicing over us with singing. By practicing mindfulness, we can cultivate a continual awareness of God's presence, experiencing His love and guidance throughout our DAY. This practice helps us stay connected to God, allows us to find solace in His presence, and helps us live with a profound sense of purpose and joy. Mindfulness in God's presence allows us to experience His peace and grace in every moment.

Prayer:

Heavenly Father, help me to live mindfully in Your presence and to be aware of Your constant companionship. Teach me to find joy and comfort in Your love and to walk closely with You each DAY. Amen.

AUGUST 26

Mindfulness and Worship

Bible Verse:

"God is spirit, and his worshipers must worship in the Spirit and in truth." — John 4:24 (MSG)

Commentary:

Mindfulness in worship involves being fully present and engaged in our worship of God. John 4:24 calls us to worship in Spirit and truth, emphasizing the importance of sincerity and attentiveness in our worship and praise. By focusing our thoughts and hearts on God during worship, we can connect with Him more deeply and experience His presence more fully. Mindful worship helps us express our love and gratitude to God, drawing us closer to Him and enhancing our spiritual growth.

Prayer:

Lord, help me to practice mindfulness in worship and to worship You in Spirit and truth. Teach me to be fully present in my praise and to connect with You deeply in my worship. Amen.

The Power of Stillness

Bible Verse:

"Be still before the Lord and wait patiently for him."
— Psalm 37:7 (MSG)

Commentary:

The power of stillness lies in its ability to connect us with God's peace and presence. Psalm 37:7 encourages us to be still before the Lord and to wait patiently for Him, highlighting the importance of quieting our minds and hearts. By practicing mindfulness and embracing stillness, we create space for God to speak to us, calm our worries, and fill us with His peace. Stillness allows us to rest in God's love, trust in His timing, and profoundly reflect His presence.

Prayer:

Heavenly Father, help me to embrace the power of stillness and to be still before You. Teach me to wait patiently for You and to find peace in Your presence. Amen.

AUGUST 28

Mindfulness in Spiritual Discipline

Bible Verse:

"Discipline yourself for the purpose of godliness." —
1 Timothy 4:7 (MSG)

Commentary:

Mindfulness in spiritual discipline involves being intentional and focused in our efforts to grow closer to God. 1 Timothy 4:7 calls us to discipline ourselves for the purpose of godliness, emphasizing the importance of mindful practice in our spiritual journey. By incorporating mindfulness into our spiritual disciplines, such as prayer, Bible study, fasting, and worship, we can solidify our connection with God and strengthen our faith. Mindfulness helps us stay committed to our spiritual practices and encourages us to pursue godliness with intention and purpose.

Prayer:

Lord, help me to practice mindfulness in my spiritual disciplines and to pursue godliness with intention and purpose. Teach me to grow closer to You through my spiritual practices and to honor You in all I do. Amen.

AUGUST 29

Building a Mindfulness Practice

Bible Verse:

"But seek first his kingdom and his righteousness, and all these things will be given to you as well." — Matthew 6:33 (MSG)

Commentary:

Building a mindfulness practice involves making a daily commitment to live with intention and focus on God. Matthew 6:33 encourages us to seek God's kingdom first, reminding us of the importance of prioritizing our spiritual growth. Habitual practice of mindfulness can include setting aside time for prayer, meditation, deep breathing, and reflection. By establishing a routine that integrates mindfulness into our lives, we can cultivate a deeper awareness of God's presence, reduce stress, and enhance our spiritual journey.

Prayer:

Heavenly Father, help me to build a mindfulness practice that seeks Your kingdom first. Teach me to establish a daily routine that fosters a deeper awareness of Your presence and nurtures my spiritual growth. Amen.

AUGUST 30

Overcoming Challenges to Mindfulness

Bible Verse:

"I can do all this through him who gives me strength." — Philippians 4:13 (MSG)

Commentary:

Overcoming challenges to mindfulness requires relying on God's strength and perseverance. Philippians 4:13 reminds us that we can do all things through Christ who strengthens us, including maintaining a mindful lifestyle despite distractions and challenges. Whether it's a hectic schedule, stress, or wandering thoughts, mindfulness can be difficult to sustain. By leaning on God for strength and focusing on His presence, we can overcome these obstacles and stay committed to our mindfulness practice.

Prayer:

Lord, help me to overcome challenges to mindfulness and to rely on Your strength. Teach me to stay focused and committed to my practice, trusting in Your guidance and grace. Amen.

AUGUST 31

Commitment to Mindful Living

Bible Verse:

"Let us not become weary in doing good, for at the proper time we will reap a harvest if we do not give up." — Galatians 6:9 (MSG)

Commentary:

A commitment to mindful living involves dedicating ourselves to a lifestyle of awareness, intention, and spiritual growth. Galatians 6:9 encourages us not to become weary in doing good, promising that we will reap a harvest if we do not give up. By choosing to live each DAY mindfully, we commit to a journey of continuous growth, deeper connection with God, and intentional and goal-oriented living. Mindful living helps us stay present, reduce stress, and experience God's peace and joy more fully.

Prayer:

Heavenly Father, help me to commit to a mindful lifestyle and not grow weary in doing good. Teach me to live each DAY with intention, awareness, and dedication to You, reaping the harvest of a life well-lived in Your presence. Amen.

WELCOME TO THE MONTH OF SEPTEMBER – THEME: PERSONAL GROWTH AND LIFE GOALS

SEPTEMBER 1

Understanding Personal Growth

Bible Verse:

"But grow in the grace and knowledge of our Lord and Savior Jesus Christ. To him be glory both now and forever! Amen"— 2 Peter 3:18 (MSG)

Commentary:

Understanding personal growth involves recognizing it as a continual process of developing into the person God intends you to be. 2 Peter 3:18 encourages us to grow in grace and knowledge, highlighting that personal growth is a journey of becoming more like Christ. It encompasses spiritual, emotional, mental, and physical development. By focusing on personal growth, we commit to ongoing transformation, allowing God to shape us through experiences, learning, and His Word. This growth helps us live more purposefully and aligns us with God's will for our lives.

Prayer:

Lord, help me to understand the importance of personal growth. Teach me to embrace this journey with a heart open to Your guidance, growing in grace and knowledge each day. Amen.

SEPTEMBER 2

Creating a Growth Plan

Bible Verse:

"Commit to the Lord whatever you do, and he will establish your plans." — Proverbs 16:3 (MSG)

Commentary:

Creating a growth plan involves setting clear intentions and goals for your personal development. Proverbs 16:3 reminds us to commit our actions to the Lord, trusting that He will guide and establish our plans. A growth plan helps us focus on areas where we need improvement and sets a blueprint for achieving our goals. By prayerfully creating a plan, we invite God into our growth journey, allowing Him to direct our steps and bring about the transformation He desires in us.

Prayer:

Heavenly Father, help me to create a growth plan that aligns with Your will. Teach me to commit my plans to You, trusting that You will guide my steps and establish my path. Amen.

SEPTEMBER 3

Identifying Your Core Values

Bible Verse:

"Above all else, guard your heart, for everything you do flows from it." — Proverbs 4:23 (MSG)

Commentary:

Identifying your core values is essential for guiding your personal growth and decision-making. Proverbs 4:23 advises us to guard our hearts, emphasizing that our values shape our actions and attitudes. Core values are the fundamental beliefs that drive your behavior and choices. By identifying and aligning with your values, you create a solid foundation for growth that reflects your true self and God's principles. Understanding your core values helps you stay focused and make decisions that honor God and support your personal development.

Prayer:

Lord, help me to identify and align with my core values. Teach me to guard my heart and to live in a way that reflects Your principles and brings honor to Your name. Amen.

SEPTEMBER 4

The Role of Faith in Personal Growth

Bible Verse:

"And without faith, it is impossible to please God, because anyone who comes to him must believe that he exists and that he rewards those who earnestly seek him." — Hebrews 11:6 (MSG)

Commentary:

Faith plays a pivotal role in personal growth, serving as the foundation for all spiritual development. Hebrews 11:6 teaches that without faith, it is impossible to please God, underscoring the importance of believing in His presence and promises. Faith allows us to trust God's guidance, rely on His strength, and believe in His plans for our transformation. By cultivating faith, we open ourselves to God's transforming power, enabling us to grow spiritually and fulfill His purpose for our lives.

Prayer:

Heavenly Father, help me to cultivate faith in my personal growth journey. Teach me to trust in Your guidance, rely on Your strength, and believe in Your promises as I seek to grow in You. Amen.

SEPTEMBER 5

Assessing Your Current Path

Bible Verse:

"Examine yourselves to see whether you are in the faith; test yourselves. Do you not realize that Christ Jesus is in you—unless, of course, you fail the test?"
— 2 Corinthians 13:5 (MSG)

Commentary:

Assessing your current path involves reflecting on your life to determine if it aligns with your values, goals, and God's purpose. 2 Corinthians 13:5 encourages us to examine ourselves to ensure we are living in faith. By regularly assessing our progress and making adjustments as needed, we can stay on track toward personal growth. This practice helps us identify areas where we need improvement and strengthens our commitment to living a life that reflects God's will.

Prayer:

Lord, help me to assess my current path with honesty and humility. Teach me to examine my life in light of Your truth and to make adjustments that align with Your purpose for me. Amen

SEPTEMBER 6

Building a Growth Mindset

Bible Verse:

"Do not conform to the pattern of this world, but be transformed by the renewing of your mind. Then you will be able to test and approve what God's will is—his good, pleasing and perfect will." — Romans 12:2 (MSG)

Commentary:

Building a growth mindset involves cultivating an attitude of continuous learning and openness to change. Romans 12:2 urges us not to conform to the world but to be transformed by renewing our minds. A growth mindset embraces challenges, learns from mistakes, and views effort as a path to mastery. By renewing our minds with God's truth and focusing on personal development, we align ourselves with God's will and prepare for His transformative work in our lives.

Prayer:

Heavenly Father, help me build a growth mindset that is open to learning and transformation. Teach me to renew my mind with Your truth and to seek Your will in all areas of my life. Amen.

SEPTEMBER 7

Overcoming Fear of Change

Bible Verse:

"For God has not given us a spirit of fear, but of power and of love and of a sound mind." — 2 Timothy 1:7 (MSG)

Commentary:

Overcoming the fear of change is vital for embracing personal growth and reaching your potential. 2 Timothy 1:7 reminds us that God has not given us a spirit of fear but one of power, love, and a sound mind. Fear of change can hold us back from pursuing new opportunities and experiences contributing to our growth. By trusting in God's strength and love, we can face change with courage and confidence, knowing He is with us in every walk of life.

Prayer:

Lord, help me to overcome the fear of change and to embrace the growth You have for me. Teach me to trust in Your power, love, and wisdom with courage and confidence as I step into new opportunities. Amen.

SEPTEMBER 8

Setting Achievable Goals

Bible Verse:

"The plans of the diligent lead to profit as surely as haste leads to poverty." — Proverbs 21:5 (MSG)

Commentary:

Setting achievable goals is crucial for ensuring steady progress in your personal growth journey. Proverbs 21:5 reminds us that diligent planning leads to success, while haste often results in failure. Setting achievable goals is important to be realistic about your current abilities, resources, and time. Break down larger objectives into smaller, manageable steps, and create a timeline for reaching each milestone. Setting attainable goals creates a clear path forward, encouraging motivation and persistence in your growth journey.

Prayer:

Heavenly Father, help me set achievable goals aligning with Your will for my life. Teach me to plan diligently and to trust in Your guidance as I pursue my personal growth journey. Amen.

SEPTEMBER 9

Aligning Your Goals with God's Purpose

Bible Verse:

"For I know the plans I have for you," declares the Lord, "plans to prosper you and not to harm you, plans to give you hope and a future." — Jeremiah 29:11 (MSG)

Commentary:

Aligning your goals with God's purpose ensures that your growth journey is guided by His wisdom and love. Jeremiah 29:11 reminds us that God has plans for our prosperity and hope. By seeking God's direction in setting our goals, we align our desires with His will, allowing Him to lead us toward the future He has prepared for us. This alignment not only brings peace and clarity but also helps us focus on what truly matters, fostering growth that honors God and serves His kingdom.

Prayer:

Lord, help me to align my goals with Your purpose for my life. Teach me to seek Your guidance and trust in your plans for me, knowing that You have a future full of hope. Amen.

SEPTEMBER 10

Breaking Down Long-Term Goals

Bible Verse:

"The heart of man plans his way, but the Lord establishes his steps." — Proverbs 16:9 (MSG)

Commentary:

Breaking down long-term goals into smaller, actionable steps makes them more manageable and attainable. Proverbs 16:9 acknowledges that while we may plan our paths, it is the Lord who directs our steps. By dividing a larger goal into smaller tasks, we can focus on each step, making steady progress without feeling overwhelmed. This approach allows us to celebrate small victories along the way and maintain momentum toward achieving our long-term objectives, trusting that God will guide us through each step.

Prayer:

Heavenly Father, help me to break down my long-term goals into manageable steps. Teach me to trust in Your guidance as I take each step forward, knowing that You are establishing my path. Amen.

Creating a Vision Board

Bible Verse:

"Where there is no vision, the people perish; but he that keepeth the law, happy is he." — Proverbs 29:18 (KJV)

Commentary:

Creating a vision board is a powerful way to visualize your goals and keep them at the forefront of your mind. Proverbs 29:18 emphasizes the importance of vision, highlighting that a lack of direction can lead to aimlessness. A vision board helps you stay focused and motivated by providing a visual representation of your dreams and aspirations. By regularly reviewing your vision board, you can remind yourself of your goals and the steps needed to achieve them, staying inspired and committed to your growth journey.

Prayer:

Lord, help me to create a vision for my life that aligns with Your purpose. Teach me to use tools like vision boards to stay focused and motivated, keeping my eyes on the goals You have set before me. Amen.

SEPTEMBER 12

Time Management for Growth

Bible Verse:

"Teach us to number our days, that we may gain a heart of wisdom." — Psalm 90:12 (MSG)

Commentary:

Effective time management is essential for personal growth and achieving life goals. Psalm 90:12 asks God to teach us to number our days, emphasizing the importance of making the most of our time. By prioritizing tasks, setting deadlines, and minimizing distractions, we can make efficient use of our time and focus on what truly matters. Good time management allows us to balance our responsibilities, pursue our goals, and create space for rest and reflection, fostering a well-rounded growth journey.

Prayer:

Heavenly Father, teach me to manage my time wisely and to prioritize my growth journey. Help me to make the most of each DAY, using my time to pursue the goals You have set before me. Amen.

SEPTEMBER 13

Tracking Your Progress

Bible Verse:

"The path of the righteous is like the morning sun, shining ever brighter till the full light of day." — Proverbs 4:18 (MSG)

Commentary:

Tracking your progress is crucial for staying on course and measuring growth over time. Proverbs 4:18 compares the path of the righteous to the morning sun, gradually shining brighter. By regularly reviewing your goals and reflecting on your progress, you can identify areas for improvement and celebrate your achievements. Keeping track of your growth helps you stay motivated, maintain focus, and make necessary adjustments, ensuring steady progress toward your life goals.

Prayer:

Lord, help me to track my progress and to stay focused on my growth journey with determination. Teach me to reflect on my achievements and to learn from my experiences, shining ever brighter in Your light. Amen.

Celebrating Small Wins

Bible Verse:

"Rejoice in the Lord always. I will say it again: Rejoice!" — Philippians 4:4 (MSG)

Commentary:

Celebrating small wins is important for maintaining motivation and recognizing progress. Philippians 4:4 encourages us to rejoice in the Lord always, reminding us to find joy in all circumstances. Acknowledging even the smallest achievements helps us stay positive and motivated, reinforcing our commitment to our goals. Celebrating small wins encourages us to keep moving forward, fostering a sense of accomplishment and gratitude for the growth we've experienced.

Prayer:

Heavenly Father, help me to celebrate the small wins in my growth journey. Teach me to find joy in each step forward and be grateful to You for my progress. Amen.

SEPTEMBER 15

The Power of Daily Habits

Bible Verse:

"Whoever can be trusted with very little can also be trusted with much, and whoever is dishonest with very little will also be dishonest with much." — Luke 16:10 (MSG)

Commentary:

The power of daily habits lies in their ability to shape our character and lead us toward success. Luke 16:10 reminds us that faithfulness in small things leads to trustworthiness in bigger things. By developing positive daily habits, such as prayer, exercise, or reading Scripture, we establish a strong foundation for personal growth. Consistent habits help us build discipline, stay focused on our goals, and develop a lifestyle that honors God. These small, everyday practices accumulate over time, leading to significant transformations in our lives.

Prayer:

Lord, help me to cultivate daily habits that honor You and lead to personal growth. Teach me to be faithful in the small things, knowing they will lead to greater trust and success in my journey. Amen.

SEPTEMBER 16

Establishing a Morning Routine

Bible Verse:

"In the morning, Lord, you hear my voice; in the morning, I lay my requests before you and wait expectantly." — Psalm 5:3 (MSG)

Commentary:

Establishing a morning routine sets a positive tone for the rest of the DAY. Psalm 5:3 highlights the practice of starting the DAY with prayer, laying our requests before God, and waiting expectantly. A morning routine that includes time for prayer, meditation, exercise, or goal-setting helps us begin each DAY with intention and focus. By dedicating the first moments of our DAY to God and our growth, we prepare our hearts and minds for the challenges and opportunities ahead, fostering a sense of peace and purpose.

Prayer:

Heavenly Father, help me to establish a morning routine that sets the tone for a productive and intentional DAY. Teach me to start each morning with You, seeking Your guidance and strength for the DAY ahead. Amen.

SEPTEMBER 17

Creating Healthy Boundaries

Bible Verse:

"Above all else, guard your heart, for everything you do flows from it." — Proverbs 4:23 (MSG)

Commentary:

Healthy boundaries are essential for protecting our well-being and focusing on our growth goals. Proverbs 4:23 emphasizes the importance of guarding our hearts, as everything we do flows from them. Setting boundaries involves knowing our limits, saying no to distractions, and prioritizing our needs and values. Healthy boundaries help us maintain balance, avoid burnout, and protect our time and energy for the things that matter most. Establishing boundaries creates a safe space for personal growth and spiritual development.

Prayer:

Lord, help me to create healthy boundaries that protect my well-being and honor You. Teach me to guard my heart and to focus on the things that lead to growth and fulfillment. Amen.

SEPTEMBER 18

Prioritizing Self-Care

Bible Verse:

"Do you not know that your bodies are temples of the Holy Spirit, who is in you, whom you have received from God? You are not your own." — 1 Corinthians 6:19 (MSG)

Commentary:

Prioritizing self-care is crucial for sustaining personal growth and maintaining a healthy lifestyle. 1 Corinthians 6:19 reminds us that our bodies are temples of the Holy Spirit, emphasizing the importance of caring for ourselves. Self-care involves resting, nourishing our bodies, and nurturing our mental and emotional health. By prioritizing self-care, we honor the body God has given us and ensure we have the strength and energy to pursue our goals and serve others effectively.

Prayer:

Heavenly Father, help me to prioritize self-care and honor the body You have given me. Teach me to take time for rest and nourishment, ensuring I have the strength to grow and serve You. Amen.

SEPTEMBER 19

Patience and Perseverance

Bible Verse:

"Let perseverance finish its work so that you may be mature and complete, not lacking anything." — James 1:4 (MSG)

Commentary:

Cultivating patience and perseverance is vital for achieving long-term growth and success. James 1:4 encourages us to let perseverance complete our work, leading to maturity and completeness. Personal growth often involves challenges and setbacks, requiring patience and determination to keep moving forward. By cultivating a spirit of perseverance, we learn to trust in God's timing and remain committed to our goals, even when progress seems slow. Patience and perseverance help us build resilience, deepen our faith, and achieve lasting transformation.

Prayer:

Lord, help me to cultivate patience and perseverance in my growth journey. Teach me to trust in Your timing and to remain steadfast in my pursuit of maturity and completeness in You. Amen.

SEPTEMBER 20

Overcoming Procrastination

Bible Verse:

"Whatever your hand finds to do, do it with all your might." — Ecclesiastes 9:10 (MSG)

Commentary:

Overcoming procrastination is essential for staying productive and achieving your goals. Ecclesiastes 9:10 encourages us to do everything with all our might, emphasizing the importance of diligence and focus. Procrastination often stems from fear, perfectionism, or lack of motivation. By recognizing these triggers and developing strategies to overcome them, such as breaking tasks into smaller steps or setting deadlines, we can combat procrastination and stay on track toward our growth goals. Taking action with intention and effort leads to progress and success.

Prayer:

Heavenly Father, help me overcome procrastination and approach my tasks with diligence and focus. Teach me to take action with intention and to do everything with all my might for Your glory. Amen.

SEPTEMBER 21

Discipline and Commitment

Bible Verse:

"No discipline seems pleasant at the time but painful. Later on, however, it produces a harvest of righteousness and peace for those who have been trained by it." — Hebrews 12:11 (MSG)

Commentary:

Embracing discipline and commitment is key to achieving personal growth and reaching your goals. Hebrews 12:11 acknowledges that discipline may be challenging but ultimately leads to a harvest of righteousness and peace. Discipline involves setting boundaries, making sacrifices, and staying committed to your growth journey, even when it's difficult. By embracing discipline, we develop self-control, build resilience, and cultivate a life that reflects God's righteousness. Commitment to discipline ensures steady progress and long-term success in our personal and spiritual growth.

Prayer:

Lord, help me to embrace discipline and commitment in my growth journey. Teach me to endure challenges with faith and perseverance, trusting that they will lead to a harvest of righteousness and peace. Amen.

SEPTEMBER 22

Barriers to Growth

Bible Verse:

"Search me, God, and know my heart; test me and know my anxious thoughts." — Psalm 139:23 (MSG)

Commentary:

Identifying barriers to growth is an essential step in overcoming obstacles that hinder personal development. Psalm 139:23 invites God to search our hearts and reveal any anxieties or hidden barriers. These obstacles might include fear, doubt, past failures, or limiting beliefs. By acknowledging and addressing these barriers, we can remove the hindrances that prevent us from achieving our goals. Asking God to search our hearts and reveal any impediments allows us to confront these issues with His divine guidance and support.

Prayer:

Heavenly Father, search my heart and reveal any barriers to my growth. Help me to confront these obstacles with courage and trust in Your guidance as I pursue the path You have set before me. Amen.

SEPTEMBER 23

Learning from Failure

Bible Verse:

"For though the righteous fall seven times, they rise again, but the wicked stumble when calamity strikes." — Proverbs 24:16 (MSG)

Commentary:

Learning from failure is a crucial part of personal growth and resilience. Proverbs 24:16 encourages us to rise again after falling, highlighting the importance of perseverance. Failures and setbacks are inevitable in life, but they offer valuable lessons that can lead to growth and improvement. We can develop resilience and continue moving forward by viewing failure as an opportunity to learn and grow, rather than a defeat. Embracing failure with a positive mindset allows us to use each experience as a stepping stone toward success.

Prayer:

Lord, help me to learn from my failures and to rise again with resilience and determination. Teach me to see each setback as an opportunity for growth and to trust in Your plan for my life. Amen.

SEPTEMBER 24

Managing Stress and Burnout

Bible Verse:

"Come to me, all you who are weary and burdened, and I will give you rest." — Matthew 11:28 (MSG)

Commentary:

Managing stress and avoiding burnout is essential for sustaining personal growth and achieving life goals. Matthew 11:28 invites us to come to Jesus when we are weary, promising rest and renewal. In our pursuit of growth and success, it's easy to become overwhelmed and overworked. By recognizing the signs of stress and burnout, we can take proactive steps to rest, recharge, and seek God's peace. Prioritizing self-care and maintaining a balanced lifestyle helps us stay healthy and focused on our growth journey.

Prayer:

Heavenly Father, help me to manage stress and avoid burnout in my growth journey. Teach me to find rest in You and to prioritize self-care, ensuring I have the strength and energy to pursue my goals. Amen.

SEPTEMBER 25

Finding Inspiration in Scripture

Bible Verse:

"Your word is a lamp for my feet, a light on my path."
— Psalm 119:105 (MSG)

Commentary:

Finding inspiration in Scripture provides guidance and encouragement on our growth journey. Psalm 119:105 describes God's Word as a lamp for our feet and a light on our path, illustrating its role in guiding us through life's challenges. The Bible offers wisdom, comfort, and motivation for personal growth and spiritual development. By turning to Scripture regularly, we can find the strength, clarity, and inspiration needed to stay dedicated to our goals and overcome obstacles. God's Word serves as a constant source of encouragement and direction.

Prayer:

Lord, help me to find inspiration in Your Word as I pursue my growth journey. Teach me to rely on Scripture for guidance, strength, and encouragement, trusting in Your wisdom to light my path. Amen.

SEPTEMBER 26

Building a Support System

Bible Verse:

"Therefore encourage one another and build each other up, just as, in fact, you are doing." — 1 Thessalonians 5:11 (MSG)

Commentary:

Building a support system is vital for achieving personal growth and reaching our goals. 1 Thessalonians 5:11 encourages us to encourage one another and build each other up, emphasizing the importance of community. A strong support system includes friends, family, mentors, and spiritual leaders who provide encouragement, guidance, and accountability. Surrounding ourselves with positive influences helps us stay motivated, overcome challenges, and celebrate successes. A supportive community fosters growth, resilience, and a sense of belonging on our journey.

Prayer:

Heavenly Father, help me to build a strong support system that encourages and uplifts me in my growth journey. Teach me to seek out positive influences and to be a source of support and encouragement to others as well. Amen.

SEPTEMBER 27

Maintaining Motivation

Bible Verse:

"Let us not become weary in doing good, for at the proper time we will reap a harvest if we do not give up." — Galatians 6:9 (MSG)

Commentary:

Maintaining motivation is essential for staying focused and committed to our growth goals. Galatians 6:9 urges us not to become weary in doing good, promising that we will reap a harvest if we do not give up. Motivation can fluctuate over time, especially when faced with challenges or setbacks. By setting clear goals, celebrating small wins, and reminding ourselves of our purpose, we can stay motivated and persevere in our growth journey. Trusting in God's promise of a fruitful harvest keeps us moving forward with hope and determination.

Prayer:

Lord, help me maintain motivation and stay committed to my growth journey. Teach me to persevere in doing good, trusting in Your promise of a harvest at the proper time. Amen.

The Role of Gratitude in Growth

Bible Verse:

"Give thanks in all circumstances; for this is God's will for you in Christ Jesus." — 1 Thessalonians 5:18 (MSG)

Commentary:

The role of gratitude in growth is to keep us grounded and focused on the blessings in our lives. 1 Thessalonians 5:18 encourages us to give thanks in all circumstances, highlighting the importance of a grateful heart. Gratitude shifts our perspective from what we lack to what we have, fostering a positive mindset and motivating us to keep growing. By practicing gratitude daily, we can find joy in the journey, appreciate our progress, and remain hopeful for the future. A thankful heart enhances our growth and strengthens our faith.

Prayer:

Heavenly Father, help me to cultivate a heart of gratitude in my growth journey. Teach me to give thanks in all circumstances and to find joy in the blessings You have provided. Amen.

Reflecting on Your Growth Journey

Bible Verse:

"Remember the wonders he has done, his miracles and the judgments he pronounced." — 1 Chronicles 16:12 (MSG)

Commentary:

Reflecting on your growth journey allows you to recognize your progress and lessons learned along the way. 1 Chronicles 16:12 encourages us to remember God's works and the miracles He has performed, reminding us of His faithfulness. By taking time to reflect on your personal growth, you can celebrate your achievements, understand the challenges you've overcome, and acknowledge the ways God has guided and supported you. This practice fosters gratitude and inspires continued growth.

Prayer:

Lord, help me to reflect on my growth journey and to remember the ways You have worked in my life. Teach me to celebrate my progress, learn from my experiences, and give thanks for Your guidance and faithfulness. Amen.

SEPTEMBER 30

Planning for Future Growth

Bible Verse:

"For which of you, intending to build a tower, does not sit down first and count the cost, whether he has enough to finish it?" — Luke 14:28 (MSG)

Commentary:

Planning for future growth involves setting new goals and creating a roadmap for continued development. Luke 14:28 emphasizes the importance of planning and preparation, suggesting that we carefully consider the steps needed to achieve our goals. By evaluating where you are now and where you want to go, you can set clear, attainable objectives for the future. This process requires prayer, reflection, and seeking God's guidance to ensure your plans align with His will and purpose for your life.

Prayer:

Heavenly Father, help me to plan for future growth and to set new goals that align with Your will. Teach me to carefully consider the steps needed to achieve my objectives and to trust in Your guidance as I continue my growth journey. Amen.

WELCOME TO THE MONTH OF OCTOBER –
THEME: GRATITUDE AND APPRECIATION

OCTOBER 1

The Foundation of Gratitude

Bible Verse:

"Give thanks to the Lord, for he is good; his love endures forever." — Psalm 107:1 (MSG)

Commentary:

The foundation of gratitude lies in recognizing God's goodness and His enduring love. Psalm 107:1 calls us to give thanks to the Lord because He is good, and His love lasts forever. Gratitude begins with acknowledging who God is and what He has done for us. It is the attitude of the heart that understands every good thing comes from God. By focusing on God's goodness and steadfast love, we can cultivate a continually grateful heart, regardless of our circumstances.

Prayer:

Lord, help me to build my life on the foundation of gratitude. Teach me to give thanks for Your goodness and to remember Your love that endures forever. Amen.

OCTOBER 2

Daily Blessings

Bible Verse:

"Blessed be the Lord, who daily bears our burdens."
— Psalm 68:19 (MSG)

Commentary:

Recognizing daily blessings involves knowing how God provides for us each DAY. Psalm 68:19 reminds us that God bears our burdens daily, highlighting His constant care and provision. We cultivate a spirit of gratitude by taking time to notice the blessings in our lives—big and small. This practice helps us appreciate the everyday gifts that we often take for granted, such as the breath in our lungs, the beauty of nature, and the love of family and friends. Acknowledging these blessings fosters a grateful heart.

Prayer:

Heavenly Father, help me to recognize the daily blessings You provide. Teach me to see Your hand in all things and to give thanks for Your constant care and provision. Amen.

OCTOBER 3

Gratitude in Challenging Times

Bible Verse:

"Give thanks in all circumstances; for this is God's will for you in Christ Jesus." — 1 Thessalonians 5:18 (MSG)

Commentary:

Gratitude in challenging times is about finding reasons to be thankful even when life is difficult. 1 Thessalonians 5:18 instructs us to give thanks in all circumstances, indicating that gratitude is always God's will for us. During trials, it can be hard to see reasons to be grateful, but focusing on God's presence, His promises, and the lessons we can learn helps us maintain a thankful heart. Gratitude in adversity builds resilience, strengthens faith, and reminds us that God is with us, no matter what we face.

Prayer:

Lord, help me to find gratitude in challenging times. Teach me to trust in Your presence and to give thanks in all circumstances, knowing that You are working for my good. Amen.

OCTOBER 4

Expressing Thanks to Others

Bible Verse:

"Therefore encourage one another and build each other up, just as, in fact, you are doing." — 1 Thessalonians 5:11 (MSG)

Commentary:

Expressing thanks to others is a powerful way to build relationships and spread joy. 1 Thessalonians 5:11 encourages us to encourage one another and build each other up, which includes expressing gratitude. We acknowledge their value and strengthen our connections by taking the time to thank those around us for their kindness, support, or simply for being in our lives. Expressing thanks fosters a positive environment, uplifts others, and reflects God's love through our words and actions.

Prayer:

Heavenly Father, help me to express my gratitude to others. Teach me to recognize the blessings they bring into my life and to build them up with words of thanks and encouragement. Amen.

OCTOBER 5

Thankfulness in Prayer

Bible Verse:

"Do not be anxious about anything, but in every situation, by prayer and petition, with thanksgiving, present your requests to God." — Philippians 4:6 (MSG)

Commentary:

Thankfulness in prayer involves approaching God with a heart full of gratitude, even as we present our needs to Him. Philippians 4:6 advises us to pray with thanksgiving, which helps shift our focus from our problems to God's goodness and faithfulness. When we thank God in prayer, we acknowledge His sovereignty and express our trust in His plans. This practice brings peace, reduces anxiety, and strengthens our relationship with God. A thankful heart in prayer draws us closer to God and aligns us with His will.

Prayer:

Lord, help me to be thankful in my prayers. Teach me to approach You with a heart full of gratitude, trusting in Your goodness, and giving thanks in all things. Amen.

OCTOBER 6

The Power of a Gratitude Journal

Bible Verse:

"Write down the revelation and make it plain on tablets so that a herald may run with it." — Habakkuk 2:2 (MSG)

Commentary:

The power of a gratitude journal lies in its ability to help us remember and reflect on God's blessings. Habakkuk 2:2 emphasizes the importance of writing things down, which helps us retain and act on them. By keeping a gratitude journal, we record what we are thankful for, allowing us to see how God is at work in our lives. This practice helps us focus on the positive, fosters a spirit of thankfulness, and serves as a reminder of God's faithfulness during difficult times.

Prayer:

Heavenly Father, help me to cultivate the habit of keeping a gratitude journal. Teach me to record Your blessings and to reflect on Your faithfulness, nurturing a heart of thankfulness. Amen.

OCTOBER 7

Gratitude for God's Creation

Bible Verse:

"The heavens declare the glory of God; the skies proclaim the work of his hands." — Psalm 19:1 (MSG)

Commentary:

Gratitude for God's creation involves recognizing the beauty and wonder of the world around us as a reflection of God's glory. Psalm 19:1 tells us that the heavens declare the glory of God, reminding us that creation itself is a testimony to His greatness. By appreciating the natural world—the stars, mountains, oceans, and all living things—we express gratitude for the Creator. This practice deepens our sense of awe and wonder, helps us feel connected to God, and reminds us of His power and creativity.

Prayer:

Lord, help me to be grateful for Your creation and to see Your glory in the world around me. Teach me to appreciate the beauty of the earth and to give thanks for the wonder of Your works. Amen.

OCTOBER 8

Seeing Challenges as Opportunities

Bible Verse:

"Consider it pure joy, my brothers and sisters, whenever you face trials of many kinds, because you know that the testing of your faith produces perseverance." — James 1:2-3 (MSG)

Commentary:

Seeing challenges as opportunities involves recognizing that difficult circumstances can lead to growth and strengthen our faith. James 1:2-3 encourages us to consider it pure joy when facing trials, understanding that these moments test our faith and produce perseverance. By shifting our perspective, we can view challenges as personal and spiritual development opportunities. This mindset helps us remain thankful, even in adversity, trusting that God uses all things for our good and His glory.

Prayer:

Heavenly Father, help me to see challenges as opportunities for growth. Teach me to find joy in trials and be grateful for how You strengthen my faith through them. Amen.

OCTOBER 9

Gratitude in Relationships

Bible Verse:

"A friend loves at all times, and a brother is born for a time of adversity." — Proverbs 17:17 (MSG)

Commentary:

Gratitude in relationships involves appreciating the people God has placed in our lives and recognizing their importance. Proverbs 17:17 speaks of a friend who loves at all times and a brother born for adversity, highlighting the value of supportive relationships. By expressing gratitude for our friends and loved ones, we strengthen these bonds and show them how much we care. A thankful heart in relationships fosters love, trust, and mutual support, enhancing our connections and reflecting God's love.

Prayer:

Lord, help me to be grateful for the relationships You have blessed me with. Teach me to appreciate my friends and loved ones and to express my gratitude for their presence in my life. Amen.

OCTOBER 10

Finding Joy in the Present Moment

Bible Verse:

"This is the DAY the Lord has made; let us rejoice and be glad in it." — Psalm 118:24 (MSG)

Commentary:

Finding joy in the present moment involves appreciating the here and now and being grateful for today. Psalm 118:24 encourages us to rejoice and be glad in the DAY the Lord has made, reminding us to focus on the present. By embracing each moment with gratefulness, we foster a joyful spirit and make the most of the time we have. This practice helps us release worries about the future or regrets about the past, allowing us to fully experience the blessings of today.

Prayer:

Heavenly Father, help me to find joy in the present moment and to appreciate each DAY You have given me. Teach me to be grateful for today and to rejoice in Your blessings. Amen.

OCTOBER 11

Appreciating Your Spiritual Journey

Bible Verse:

"I thank my God every time I remember you." — Philippians 1:3 (MSG)

Commentary:

Appreciating your spiritual journey involves recognizing your growth and progress in your relationship with God. Philippians 1:3 reflects gratitude for others in their spiritual journey, showing the value of remembering and celebrating progress. By reflecting on where you started and how far you have come, you can appreciate the transformative work God has done in your life. This gratitude helps you remain committed to your growth and motivates you to continue pursuing a deeper relationship with God.

Prayer:

Lord, help me to appreciate my spiritual journey and to be grateful for the growth I have experienced. Teach me to celebrate the progress I have made and to remain committed to my relationship with You. Amen.

OCTOBER 12

Gratitude for God's Promises

Bible Verse:

"For no matter how many promises God has made, they are "Yes" in Christ. And so through him, the "Amen" is spoken by us to the glory of God." — 2 Corinthians 1:20 (MSG)

Commentary:

Gratitude for God's promises involves trusting in His faithfulness and expressing thankfulness for the assurances He has given us. 2 Corinthians 1:20 reminds us that all of God's promises are fulfilled in Christ, affirming His commitment to us. By focusing on God's promises and giving thanks for them, we reinforce our faith and find peace in His unchanging nature. This practice helps us remain hopeful and confident, knowing that God is true to His Word and will fulfill His promises in His perfect timing.

Prayer:

Heavenly Father, help me to be grateful for Your promises and to trust in Your faithfulness. Teach me to focus on Your assurances and to find peace in Your invariable nature. Amen.

OCTOBER 13

Celebrating Milestones

Bible Verse:

"Then Samuel took a stone and set it up between Mizpah and Shen. He named it Ebenezer, saying, 'Thus far the Lord has helped us.'" — 1 Samuel 7:12 (MSG)

Commentary:

Celebrating milestones involves acknowledging significant moments and achievements in our lives and expressing gratitude for God's guidance. 1 Samuel 7:12 describes Samuel setting up a stone called Ebenezer, meaning "Thus far the Lord has helped us," to commemorate God's assistance. By celebrating milestones, we recognize God's hand in our progress and give thanks for His support. This practice helps us build a sense of accomplishment, reinforces our faith, and encourages us to trust God's continued guidance in our journey.

Prayer:

Lord, help me to celebrate the milestones in my life and to be grateful for Your guidance. Teach me to recognize Your hand in my progress and to give thanks for Your support and assistance. Amen.

OCTOBER 14

Appreciating Your Unique Gifts

Bible Verse:

"Each of you should use whatever gift you have received to serve others as faithful stewards of God's grace in its various forms." — 1 Peter 4:10 (MSG)

Commentary:

Appreciating your unique gifts involves recognizing the talents and abilities God has given you and being thankful for them. 1 Peter 4:10 encourages us to use our gifts to serve others as faithful stewards of God's grace. By appreciating your unique gifts, you acknowledge God's creativity and purpose in your life. This gratitude inspires you to use your abilities for His glory and to bless others. Recognizing and valuing your gifts fosters a sense of fulfillment and motivates you to grow and develop your talents further.

Prayer:

Heavenly Father, help me to appreciate the unique gifts You have given me and to be grateful for them. Teach me to use my talents to serve others and to honor You as a faithful steward of Your grace. Amen.

OCTOBER 15

The Habit of Thankfulness

Bible Verse:

"Rejoice always, pray continually, give thanks in all circumstances; for this is God's will for you in Christ Jesus." — 1 Thessalonians 5:16-18 (MSG)

Commentary:

The habit of thankfulness involves making gratitude a consistent practice in our daily lives. 1 Thessalonians 5:16-18 calls us to always rejoice, pray, and give thanks in all circumstances, emphasizing that this is God's will for us. By cultivating a habit of thankfulness, we train ourselves to see God's blessings in every situation, fostering a positive attitude and deepening our relationship with Him. This discipline helps us remain joyful and content, regardless of our circumstances, and keeps our focus on God's goodness.

Prayer:

Lord, help me to develop the habit of thankfulness and to give thanks in all circumstances. Teach me to rejoice always and to pray continually, keeping my heart focused on Your goodness. Amen.

OCTOBER 16

Gratitude and Humility

Bible Verse:

"Humble yourselves before the Lord, and he will lift you up." — James 4:10 (MSG)

Commentary:

Gratitude and humility are closely connected, as a grateful heart recognizes that all blessings come from God. James 4:10 encourages us to humble ourselves before the Lord, promising that He will lift us up. By acknowledging that we are not self-sufficient and that everything we have is a gift from God, we cultivate humility. Gratitude helps us remember our dependence on God and keeps us humble, fostering a spirit of thankfulness and reverence for His provision and grace.

Prayer:

Heavenly Father, help me to cultivate both gratitude and humility in my heart. Teach me to recognize that all blessings come from You and to remain humble, giving thanks for Your provision and grace. Amen.

Giving Thanks in Community

Bible Verse:

"Let the message of Christ dwell among you richly as you teach and admonish one another with all wisdom through psalms, hymns, and songs from the Spirit, singing to God with gratitude in your hearts."
— Colossians 3:16 (MSG)

Commentary:

Giving thanks in the community involves sharing our gratitude with others and fostering a culture of thankfulness within our faith communities. Colossians 3:16 encourages us to let the message of Christ dwell among us richly and to express gratitude through worship and teaching. By practicing gratitude together, we strengthen our bonds, encourage one another, and create an atmosphere of joy and appreciation. Sharing our appreciation in the community helps us recognize God's work in each other's lives and builds a supportive environment of faith and encouragement.

Prayer:

Lord, help me to give thanks in the community and to encourage others with a spirit of gratitude. Teach me to foster a culture of thankfulness within my faith community, sharing the joy of Your blessings with those around me. Amen.

OCTOBER 18

Gratitude in Worship

Bible Verse:

"Enter his gates with thanksgiving and his courts with praise; give thanks to him and praise his name."
— Psalm 100:4 (MSG)

Commentary:

Gratitude in worship is an essential part of honoring God and expressing our love for Him. Psalm 100:4 calls us to enter God's gates with thanksgiving and His courts with praise, emphasizing the importance of gratitude in our worship. By approaching worship with a thankful heart, we acknowledge God's goodness and His blessings in our lives. Gratitude enhances our worship experience, deepening our connection with God and allowing us to express our love and devotion more fully.

Prayer:

Heavenly Father, help me to bring gratitude into my worship and to praise You with a thankful heart. Teach me to enter Your presence with thanksgiving, acknowledging Your goodness and blessings in my life. Amen.

OCTOBER 19

Recognizing God's Provision

Bible Verse:

"And my God will meet all your needs according to the riches of his glory in Christ Jesus." — Philippians 4:19 (MSG)

Commentary:

Recognizing God's provision involves acknowledging that He meets all our needs and expressing gratitude for His care. Philippians 4:19 assures us that God will supply all our needs according to His riches in glory. By focusing on God's provision, we cultivate a spirit of thankfulness, understanding that every good thing comes from Him. Recognizing God's care in our lives helps us develop trust in His faithfulness and fosters a deep sense of gratitude for His generosity and love.

Prayer:

Lord, help me recognize Your provision and be grateful for how You meet my needs. Teach me to trust in Your faithfulness and to give thanks for Your generous care and love. Amen.

OCTOBER 20

Gratitude for Life's Lessons

Bible Verse:

"Consider it pure joy, my brothers and sisters, whenever you face trials of many kinds, because you know that the testing of your faith produces perseverance." — James 1:2-3 (MSG)

Commentary:

Gratitude for life's lessons involves appreciating the growth and wisdom gained through challenges and experiences. James 1:2-3 encourages us to consider it pure joy when facing trials, understanding that these moments produce perseverance. By reflecting on the lessons learned through life's ups and downs, we can find gratitude for the growth they have brought us. This practice helps us see challenges as opportunities for personal and spiritual development, fostering resilience and a deeper trust in God's plan.

Prayer:

Heavenly Father, help me to be grateful for life's lessons and to find joy in the growth they bring. Teach me to appreciate the wisdom gained through challenges and to trust in Your plan for my life. Amen.

OCTOBER 21

The Transformative Power of Gratitude

Bible Verse:

"Do not be conformed to this world, but be transformed by the renewing of your mind, that you may prove what is that good and acceptable and perfect will of God." — Romans 12:2 (MSG)

Commentary:

The transformative power of gratitude lies in its ability to renew our minds and change our perspective. Romans 12:2 encourages us to be transformed by renewing our minds, aligning us with God's will. By practicing gratitude, we shift our focus from what we lack to what we have, fostering a positive attitude and a renewed outlook on life. Gratitude helps us see the good in every situation, deepening our faith and enhancing our spiritual growth. It transforms our hearts and minds, aligning us more closely with God's purpose.

Prayer:

Lord, help me experience gratitude's transformative power in my life. Teach me to renew my mind with thankfulness and to see Your good and perfect will in every situation. Amen.

OCTOBER 22

Serving Others with a Grateful Heart

Bible Verse:

"Each of you should use whatever gift you have received to serve others as faithful stewards of God's grace in its various forms." — 1 Peter 4:10 (MSG)

Commentary:

Serving others with a grateful heart involves recognizing that our talents and resources are gifts from God, meant to be shared. 1 Peter 4:10 encourages us to use our gifts to serve others as faithful stewards of God's grace. By serving with gratitude, we acknowledge God's blessings in our lives and express our thankfulness by giving back. This attitude enhances our service, making it more joyful and fulfilling. Serving others with gratitude allows us to reflect on God's love and grace, impacting lives and building His kingdom.

Prayer:

Lord, help me to serve others with a grateful heart. Teach me to recognize my gifts as blessings from You and to use them to bless others, reflecting Your love and grace. Amen.

OCTOBER 23

Gratitude for Your Past

Bible Verse:

"Remember the former things, those of long ago; I am God, and there is no other; I am God, and there is none like me." — Isaiah 46:9 (MSG)

Commentary:

Gratitude for your past involves acknowledging the experiences that have shaped you and giving thanks for God's presence throughout your journey. Isaiah 46:9 calls us to remember the former things and recognize that God is unchanging and sovereign. Reflecting on your past with gratitude helps you see how God has guided and provided for you, even in difficult times. This practice fosters a deeper appreciation for God's faithfulness and strengthens your trust in His ongoing work in your life.

Prayer:

Heavenly Father, help me be grateful for my past and remember how You have guided me. Teach me to see Your hand in every experience and to give thanks for Your faithfulness throughout my journey. Amen.

OCTOBER 24

Thankfulness for God's Guidance

Bible Verse:

"I will instruct you and teach you in the way you should go; I will counsel you with my loving eye on you." — Psalm 32:8 (MSG)

Commentary:

Thankfulness for God's guidance involves recognizing His direction in your life and expressing gratitude for His wisdom. Psalm 32:8 assures us that God will instruct and teach us, keeping His loving eye on us. By being thankful for God's guidance, we acknowledge His care and trust in His plans. This gratitude helps us stay open to His leading, knowing that He guides us with love and wisdom. Thankfulness for God's guidance strengthens our faith and encourages us to follow His path with confidence.

Prayer:

Lord, help me to be thankful for Your guidance and to trust in Your wisdom. Teach me to recognize Your direction in my life and to give thanks for Your loving counsel. Amen.

OCTOBER 25

Gratitude for Healing and Growth

Bible Verse:

"He heals the brokenhearted and binds up their wounds." — Psalm 147:3 (MSG)

Commentary:

Gratitude for healing and growth involves acknowledging God's work in restoring and transforming us. Psalm 147:3 reminds us that God heals the brokenhearted and binds up their wounds, emphasizing His compassion and care. By expressing gratitude for the healing and growth we have experienced, we recognize God's power and grace in our lives. This gratitude helps us appreciate our progress and inspires us to continue seeking God's healing and transformative work in our hearts.

Prayer:

Heavenly Father, help me to be grateful for the healing and growth You have brought into my life. Teach me to recognize Your hand in my restoration and to give thanks for Your power and grace. Amen.

Finding Contentment through Gratitude

Bible Verse:

"I know what it is to be in need, and I know what it is to have plenty. I have learned the secret of being content in any and every situation, whether well-fed or hungry, whether living in plenty or in want." — Philippians 4:12 (MSG)

Commentary:

Finding contentment through gratitude involves recognizing God's provision in all circumstances and being thankful for His blessings. Philippians 4:12 speaks of learning to be content in every situation, understanding that contentment comes from trusting in God's provision. By focusing on what we have and giving thanks for it, we cultivate a spirit of contentment. Gratitude shifts our perspective from what we lack to what we have, helping us find contentment and peace in every circumstance.

Prayer:

Lord, help me to find contentment through gratitude. Teach me to recognize Your provision in all circumstances and to be thankful for Your blessings, finding peace and satisfaction in Your care. Amen.

Sharing Your Gratitude

Bible Verse:

"Give thanks to the Lord and proclaim his greatness; let the whole world know what he has done." — Psalm 105:1 (MSG)

Commentary:

Sharing your gratitude involves openly expressing thankfulness for God's blessings and proclaiming His greatness. Psalm 105:1 encourages us to give thanks to the Lord and let the whole world know what He has done. By sharing our gratitude with others, we inspire them to recognize God's work in their own lives and encourage them to develop a thankful heart. This practice builds a community of gratitude, strengthens our faith, and spreads the joy of God's blessings.

Prayer:

Heavenly Father, help me to share my gratitude with others and to proclaim Your greatness. Teach me to be open about the blessings You have given me and to encourage others to recognize Your work in their lives. Amen.

Practicing Gratitude During Trials

Bible Verse:

"Consider it pure joy, my brothers and sisters, whenever you face trials of many kinds." — James 1:2 (MSG)

Commentary:

Practicing gratitude during trials involves finding reasons to be thankful, even in difficult situations. James 1:2 encourages us to consider it pure joy when facing trials, understanding that they lead to growth and perseverance. By choosing gratitude during hardships, we focus on God's presence and His promises rather than our struggles. This practice helps us maintain a positive attitude, strengthen our faith, and trust in God's plan, knowing that He works all things for our good.

Prayer:

Lord, help me to practice gratitude during trials and to find joy in the midst of difficulties. Teach me to trust in Your presence and promises, knowing that You are working for my good. Amen.

OCTOBER 29

Gratitude for Today

Bible Verse:

"This is the DAY the Lord has made; let us rejoice and be glad in it." — Psalm 118:24 (MSG)

Commentary:

Gratitude for today involves being thankful for the present moment and recognizing the gift of each new day. Psalm 118:24 encourages us to rejoice and be glad in the day the Lord has made, highlighting the importance of appreciating the present. By focusing on today and expressing gratitude for its opportunities and blessings, we cultivate a heart of thankfulness. This practice helps us stay grounded, live in the moment, and appreciate the beauty and potential of each day.

Prayer:

Heavenly Father, help me to be grateful for today and to rejoice in the gift of each new DAY You have given me. Teach me to appreciate the present moment and to live with a heart full of thankfulness. Amen.

OCTOBER 30

Creating a Gratitude Ritual

Bible Verse:

"Devote yourselves to prayer, being watchful and thankful." — Colossians 4:2 (MSG)

Commentary:

Creating a gratitude ritual involves establishing a regular practice of expressing thankfulness. Colossians 4:2 encourages us to be devoted to prayer, being watchful and thankful, highlighting the importance of consistent gratitude. By setting aside time each DAY to reflect on and give thanks for our blessings, we can develop a habit of gratitude that enriches our lives. This ritual helps us stay focused on God's goodness, fosters a positive mindset, and deepens our relationship with Him.

Prayer:

Lord, help me to create a gratitude ritual that keeps my heart focused on thankfulness. Teach me to devote myself to prayer and to express my gratitude regularly, nurturing a spirit of appreciation and joy. Amen.

Living a Life of Thankfulness

Bible Verse:

"Give thanks to the Lord, for he is good; his love endures forever." — Psalm 136:1 (MSG)

Commentary:

Living a life of thankfulness involves consistently expressing gratitude and recognizing God's goodness in every aspect of life. Psalm 136:1 reminds us to give thanks to the Lord because He is good, and His love endures forever. By making gratitude a central part of our daily lives, we align our hearts with God's will and reflect His love to others. This practice helps us remain positive, content, and grounded in faith, even in challenging times. A life of thankfulness honors God and brings joy and peace to our hearts.

Prayer:

Heavenly Father, help me to live a life of thankfulness and to give thanks for Your goodness and enduring love. Teach me to recognize Your blessings in every aspect of my life and to express my gratitude daily. Amen.

WELCOME TO THE MONTH OF NOVEMBER – THEME: HEALING AND FORGIVENESS

NOVEMBER 1

Understanding Healing

Bible Verse:

"He heals the brokenhearted and binds up their wounds." — Psalm 147:3 (MSG)

Commentary:

Understanding healing involves recognizing that it is a process of restoration and renewal that encompasses our entire being—mind, body, and spirit. Psalm 147:3 reminds us that God is the healer of the brokenhearted and the One who binds up our wounds. Healing is not just about recovering from physical ailments but also about emotional and spiritual restoration. It requires patience, faith, and a willingness to allow God to work in our lives, transforming our pain into peace and strength.

Prayer:

Lord, help me to understand the full scope of Your healing power. Teach me to trust in Your ability to heal my heart and bind up my wounds. Amen.

NOVEMBER 2

Embracing Vulnerability

Bible Verse:

"But he said to me, 'My grace is sufficient for you, for my power is made perfect in weakness.'" — 2 Corinthians 12:9 (MSG)

Commentary:

Embracing vulnerability is a vital step in the healing process, as it requires us to acknowledge our weaknesses and depend on God's strength. 2 Corinthians 12:9 tells us that God's grace is sufficient and that His power is perfected in our weakness. When we allow ourselves to be vulnerable, we open our hearts to God's healing touch. Vulnerability is not a sign of weakness but a pathway to strength and healing, as it enables us to receive God's grace and love more fully.

Prayer:

Heavenly Father, help me embrace vulnerability and lean on Your strength. Teach me to find healing in my weaknesses through Your grace. Amen.

NOVEMBER 3

Letting Go of Hurt

Bible Verse:

"Forget the former things; do not dwell on the past. See, I am doing a new thing!" — Isaiah 43:18-19 (MSG)

Commentary:

Letting go of hurt is essential for moving forward in the healing journey. Isaiah 43:18-19 encourages us not to dwell on the past but to recognize the new things God is doing in our lives. Holding onto past hurts can hinder our growth and prevent us from experiencing God's renewal. By choosing to let go of pain and resentment, we make room for healing and transformation. Trusting in God's plan for a new beginning allows us to release the past and embrace a hope-filled future.

Prayer:

Lord, help me to let go of past hurts and to trust in the new things You are doing in my life. Teach me to release pain and embrace Your healing and transformation. Amen.

NOVEMBER 4

The Power of Forgiveness

Bible Verse:

"Be kind and compassionate to one another, forgiving each other, just as in Christ God forgave you." — Ephesians 4:32 (MSG)

Commentary:

The power of forgiveness lies in its ability to bring freedom and healing to our hearts and relationships. Ephesians 4:32 reminds us to forgive others just as God has forgiven us through Christ. Forgiveness is not about condoning wrongs but about releasing the burden of bitterness and allowing healing to take place. When we forgive, we open ourselves to God's grace and create space for restoration. Forgiveness heals our hearts and the bonds we share with others, fostering reconciliation and peace.

Prayer:

Heavenly Father, help me to understand the power of forgiveness and to extend grace to others. Teach me to forgive as You have forgiven me, bringing healing and freedom to my heart. Amen.

NOVEMBER 5

Healing Through Prayer

Bible Verse:

"Is anyone among you in trouble? Let them pray. Is anyone happy? Let them sing songs of praise." — James 5:13 (MSG)

Commentary:

Healing through prayer involves turning to God in times of need and trusting in His ability to heal and restore. James 5:13 encourages us to pray when we are in trouble, recognizing prayer as a powerful tool for healing. Through prayer, we communicate our pain and struggles to God, inviting His presence and intervention in our lives. Prayer connects us with God's peace and comfort, helping us release our burdens and experience His healing touch. It is a source of strength and renewal, guiding us on our journey to wholeness.

Prayer:

Lord, help me to seek healing through prayer and to trust in Your power to restore. Teach me to turn to You in times of need and to find comfort and strength in Your presence. Amen.

NOVEMBER 6

Finding Peace in God's Presence

Bible Verse:

"The Lord gives strength to his people; the Lord blesses his people with peace." — Psalm 29:11 (MSG)

Commentary:

Finding peace in God's presence is crucial to the healing journey, as it allows us to rest in His love and care. Psalm 29:11 assures us that the Lord gives strength and peace to His people. By spending time in God's presence through prayer, worship, and reflection, we open our hearts to His calming influence. This peace surpasses all understanding, providing comfort and healing amid life's challenges. In God's presence, we find rest for our souls and the strength to continue our journey toward wholeness.

Prayer:

Heavenly Father, help me to find peace in Your presence and to rest in Your love and care. Teach me to seek You in times of trouble and to trust in Your peace that heals and restores. Amen.

NOVEMBER 7

Healing Through Scripture

Bible Verse:

"Your word is a lamp for my feet, a light on my path."
— Psalm 119:105 (MSG)

Commentary:

Healing through Scripture involves immersing ourselves in God's Word, allowing it to guide and restore us. Psalm 119:105 describes God's Word as a lamp for our feet and a light on our path, highlighting its role in illuminating our lives. Meditating on Scripture provides comfort, wisdom, and encouragement for our healing journey. God's promises and teachings provide a foundation of hope and strength, helping us navigate challenges and experience His healing touch. Scripture renews our minds and transforms our hearts, drawing us closer to God.

Prayer:

Lord, help me to seek healing through Your Word and to find comfort and guidance in Scripture. Teach me to meditate on Your promises and to trust in Your wisdom and love. Amen.

NOVEMBER 8

The Gift of Forgiveness

Bible Verse:

"For if you forgive other people when they sin against you, your heavenly Father will also forgive you." — Matthew 6:14 (MSG)

Commentary:

The gift of forgiveness is a powerful act that releases both the forgiver and the forgiven from the burden of sin and resentment. Matthew 6:14 teaches us that when we forgive others, we also open ourselves to receive God's forgiveness. Forgiveness is not just a gift to others but a profound blessing for ourselves. It frees us from the chains of anger and bitterness, allowing healing and peace to enter our hearts. We align ourselves with God's grace and mercy by choosing to forgive.

Prayer:

Lord, help me to embrace the gift of forgiveness and to extend grace to others as You have extended it to me. Teach me to release resentment and to find freedom in Your forgiveness. Amen.

NOVEMBER 9

Forgiving Others

Bible Verse:

"Bear with each other and forgive one another if any of you has a grievance against someone. Forgive as the Lord forgave you." — Colossians 3:13 (MSG)

Commentary:

Forgiving others is a crucial step toward healing and reconciliation. Colossians 3:13 encourages us to forgive as the Lord has forgiven us, emphasizing the importance of extending grace to those who have wronged us. Holding onto grudges can prevent us from experiencing true freedom and peace. By forgiving others, we let go of the desire for revenge and allow God's love to heal our wounds. This act of forgiveness fosters spiritual growth, restores relationships, and reflects the heart of Christ.

Prayer:

Heavenly Father, help me to forgive others as You have forgiven me. Teach me to release anger and resentment and to embrace Your love and grace in my relationships. Amen.

NOVEMBER 10

Forgiving Yourself

Bible Verse:

"As far as the east is from the west, so far has he removed our transgressions from us." — Psalm 103:12 (MSG)

Commentary:

Forgiving yourself is essential to the healing process and accepting God's grace. Psalm 103:12 reminds us that God has removed our transgressions as far as the East is from the West, indicating complete forgiveness. Holding onto guilt and shame can hinder our spiritual growth and prevent us from experiencing God's peace. By forgiving ourselves, we accept God's forgiveness and allow His healing to transform our hearts. Self-forgiveness is a step toward freedom, self-compassion, and a deeper relationship with God.

Prayer:

Lord, help me forgive myself and accept Your grace and mercy. Teach me to release guilt and shame and embrace the freedom from Your forgiveness. Amen.

The Role of Compassion in Forgiveness

Bible Verse:

"Be kind and compassionate to one another, forgiving each other, just as in Christ God forgave you." — Ephesians 4:32 (MSG)

Commentary:

The role of compassion in forgiveness involves understanding and empathizing with others, which paves the way for genuine forgiveness. Ephesians 4:32 encourages us to be kind and compassionate, forgiving as God forgave us in Christ. Compassion allows us to see beyond the hurt and recognize the humanity of those who have wronged us. By cultivating a compassionate heart, we can extend forgiveness more freely and sincerely, fostering healing and reconciliation in our relationships.

Prayer:

Heavenly Father, help me to develop a compassionate heart and to forgive others as You have forgiven me. Teach me to see others through Your eyes and to extend grace and understanding. Amen.

NOVEMBER 12

Letting Go of Resentment

Bible Verse:

"Do not let the sun go down while you are still angry, and do not give the devil a foothold." — Ephesians 4:26-27 (MSG)

Commentary:

Letting go of resentment is crucial for healing and maintaining spiritual well-being. Ephesians 4:26-27 warns us not to let the sun go down while we are still angry, highlighting the importance of resolving conflicts quickly. Resentment can fester and grow, creating bitterness and division. By choosing to let go of anger and resentment, we protect our hearts from negativity and create space for peace and healing. This decision helps us break free from the chains of unforgiveness and move forward in grace.

Prayer:

Lord, help me to let go of resentment and to resolve conflicts quickly. Teach me to release anger and bitterness and to embrace Your peace and healing in my heart. Amen.

NOVEMBER 13

Forgiveness Without Reconciliation

Bible Verse:

"If it is possible, as far as it depends on you, live at peace with everyone." — Romans 12:18 (MSG)

Commentary:

Forgiveness without reconciliation acknowledges that while we are called to forgive, reconciliation may not always be possible or healthy. Romans 12:18 advises us to live at peace with everyone as much as it depends on us, recognizing that peace may not always involve restored relationships. Forgiveness is about releasing the burden of anger and finding peace within ourselves, regardless of the other person's actions. It frees us from the bondage of bitterness and allows us to heal, even if reconciliation is not feasible.

Prayer:

Heavenly Father, help me to forgive even when reconciliation is not possible. Teach me to release the burden of anger and to find peace in Your grace and love. Amen.

NOVEMBER 14

Choosing Forgiveness Daily

Bible Verse:

"Then Peter came to Jesus and asked, 'Lord, how many times shall I forgive my brother or sister who sins against me? Up to seven times?' Jesus answered, 'I tell you, not seven times, but seventy-seven times.'" — Matthew 18:21-22 (MSG)

Commentary:

Choosing compassion and forgiveness daily means continually deciding to forgive, even when it's difficult. Matthew 18:21-22 illustrates that forgiveness is not a one-time act but a repeated choice, emphasizing the need to forgive without limit. This daily commitment to forgiveness helps us maintain a heart free from bitterness and resentment, allowing God's love to flow through us. By choosing to forgive repeatedly, we align ourselves with God's heart and experience the freedom and healing that come from living in His grace.

Prayer:

Lord, help me to choose forgiveness daily, even when it's difficult. Teach me to forgive without limit and to keep my heart free from bitterness, embracing Your grace and love. Amen.

Mental Healing and Renewal

Bible Verse:

"Do not conform to the pattern of this world, but be transformed by the renewing of your mind. Then you will be able to test and approve what God's will is—his good, pleasing and perfect will." — Romans 12:2 (MSG)

Commentary:

Mental healing and renewal involve transforming and aligning our thoughts with God's truth. Romans 12:2 encourages us to renew our minds, which is key to experiencing transformation and discerning God's will. Negative thought patterns can hinder our growth and keep us trapped in past hurts. By focusing on God's Word and allowing it to reshape our thinking, we can experience mental healing and find peace. Renewing our minds helps us break free from harmful beliefs and embrace the truth of who we are in Christ.

Prayer:

Lord, help me to experience mental healing and renewal through Your Word. Teach me to transform my thoughts and align them with Your truth, finding peace and freedom in Your presence. Amen.

NOVEMBER 16

Emotional Healing

Bible Verse:

"He heals the brokenhearted and binds up their wounds." — Psalm 147:3 (MSG)

Commentary:

Emotional healing is a vital part of the journey toward wholeness. Psalm 147:3 reassures us that God heals the brokenhearted and binds up their wounds, offering comfort and restoration. Emotional pain can be deep and long-lasting, but God's healing touch can bring relief and renewal. We invite God into our healing journey by allowing ourselves to feel and process our emotions. Surrendering our hurts to God and seeking His comfort helps us recover from emotional wounds and grow stronger in faith.

Prayer:

Heavenly Father, help me to experience emotional healing through Your love and grace. Teach me to surrender my pain to You and to trust in Your ability to heal and restore my heart. Amen.

NOVEMBER 17

Physical Healing

Bible Verse:

"Is anyone among you sick? Let them call the elders of the church to pray over them and anoint them with oil in the name of the Lord." — James 5:14 (MSG)

Commentary:

Physical healing is essential to overall well-being. God cares about our physical health and instructs us to be mindful of our bodies and souls. James 5:14 encourages us to seek prayer and anointing for healing when we are unwell, reminding us that God is the ultimate healer. While we should seek medical care, we must also remember that God is with us in our physical struggles. By praying to God and seeking His healing, we acknowledge His power and trust in His ability to restore our bodies.

Prayer:

Lord, help me to seek physical healing through prayer and trust in Your power to restore. Teach me to turn to You in my physical struggles and to believe in Your healing touch. Amen.

NOVEMBER 18

Healing from Trauma

Bible Verse:

"The Lord is close to the brokenhearted and saves those who are crushed in spirit." — Psalm 34:18 (MSG)

Commentary:

Healing from trauma involves acknowledging the pain and seeking God's comfort and restoration. Psalm 34:18 reminds us that God is close to the brokenhearted and saves those who are crushed in spirit, offering hope to those who have experienced deep wounds. Trauma can leave lasting scars, but God's love and grace can heal even the most profound hurts. We can find restoration and peace by seeking God's presence, sharing our pain with trusted individuals, and allowing ourselves to heal gradually.

Prayer:

Heavenly Father, help me to heal from trauma and to find comfort in Your presence. Teach me to seek Your love and grace and to trust in Your ability to restore my heart and spirit. Amen.

The Role of Community in Healing

Bible Verse:

"Carry each other's burdens, and in this way, you will fulfill the law of Christ." — Galatians 6:2 (MSG)

Commentary:

The role of community in healing is essential, as it provides support, encouragement, and accountability. Galatians 6:2 encourages us to carry each other's burdens, highlighting the importance of community in our healing journey. Sharing our struggles with trusted friends or family members can bring comfort and strength. A supportive community helps us feel less isolated and offers a safe space to heal. By leaning on others and allowing them to support us, we experience God's love through the care and compassion of our community.

Prayer:

Lord, help me to find healing through community and to lean on the support of others. Teach me to carry each other's burdens and to experience Your love through the care of those around me. Amen.

NOVEMBER 20

Spiritual Healing Through Worship

Bible Verse:

"Come, let us bow down in worship, let us kneel before the Lord, our Maker; for he is our God and we are the people of his pasture, the flock under his care." — Psalm 95:6-7 (MSG)

Commentary:

Spiritual healing through worship involves connecting with God and allowing His presence to bring renewal. Psalm 95:6-7 invites us to bow down in worship and kneel before God, recognizing that we are under His care. Worship is a powerful way to experience God's healing, as it shifts our focus from our pain to His greatness. We encounter God's presence through worship, which brings comfort, peace, and restoration. Worship helps us surrender our burdens to God and receive His healing touch in our spirits.

Prayer:

Heavenly Father, help me to find spiritual healing through worship and to connect with You deeply. Teach me to bow before You in surrender and to receive Your healing and restoration in my spirit. Amen.

NOVEMBER 21

Healing Through Meditation and Reflection

Bible Verse:

"I will meditate on your precepts and consider your ways." — Psalm 119:15 (MSG)

Commentary:

Healing through meditation and reflection involves taking time to ponder God's Word and His ways, allowing them to transform our hearts. Psalm 119:15 speaks of meditating on God's precepts and considering His ways, highlighting the importance of reflection in our spiritual journey. By meditating on Scripture and reflecting on God's promises, we find comfort, guidance, and healing. This practice helps us align our thoughts with God's truth and opens our hearts to His healing presence, bringing renewal and peace.

Prayer:

Lord, help me to find healing through meditation and reflection on Your Word. Teach me to ponder Your precepts and consider Your ways, experiencing comfort and renewal in Your presence. Amen.

NOVEMBER 22

Practicing Grace and Mercy

Bible Verse:

"The Lord is compassionate and gracious, slow to anger, abounding in love." — Psalm 103:8 (MSG)

Commentary:

Practicing grace and mercy involves extending the same kindness and understanding to others that God extends to us. Psalm 103:8 reminds us that the Lord is compassionate and gracious, setting an example for us to follow. By practicing grace, we choose to forgive and release others from the weight of their mistakes. Mercy goes hand in hand with grace, showing compassion even when it is not deserved. When we embody grace and mercy, we create a foundation for forgiveness and healing in our relationships.

Prayer:

Lord, help me to practice grace and mercy in my daily life. Teach me to be compassionate and forgiving, just as You have shown grace and mercy to me. Amen.

NOVEMBER 23

Recognizing the Need for Forgiveness

Bible Verse:

"Create in me a pure heart, O God, and renew a steadfast spirit within me." — Psalm 51:10 (MSG)

Commentary:

Recognizing the need for forgiveness is the first step in healing and restoration. Psalm 51:10 is a prayer for a pure heart and a renewed spirit, acknowledging our need for God's forgiveness and grace. Examining our hearts and acknowledging where we have wronged others, or ourselves opens the door for God's cleansing and renewal. Recognizing the need for forgiveness allows us to take responsibility for our actions, seek God's grace, and begin the process of healing.

Prayer:

Heavenly Father, help me to recognize the need for forgiveness in my life. Teach me to examine my heart and to seek Your grace and renewal. Amen.

Overcoming Bitterness

Bible Verse:

"Get rid of all bitterness, rage and anger, brawling and slander, along with every form of malice." — Ephesians 4:31 (MSG)

Commentary:

Overcoming bitterness is essential for experiencing true freedom and peace. Ephesians 4:31 encourages us to get rid of bitterness, rage, anger, and malice, which can poison our hearts and hinder our growth. Bitterness often stems from unresolved hurt and unforgiveness, keeping us stuck in a cycle of pain. By forgiving and releasing bitterness, we free ourselves from its destructive power and open our hearts to healing and restoration. Letting go of bitterness allows us to fully experience God's peace and joy.

Prayer:

Lord, help me to overcome bitterness and to let go of anger and resentment. Teach me to release my hurts to You and to find freedom and peace in Your love. Amen.

Learning from Jesus' Example

Bible Verse:

"Father, forgive them, for they do not know what they are doing." — Luke 23:34 (MSG)

Commentary:

Learning from Jesus' example teaches us the power of forgiveness, even in the face of great suffering. Luke 23:34 records Jesus' words on the cross, asking God to forgive those who were crucifying Him. This profound act of forgiveness shows us that forgiveness is a choice, regardless of the offense. Jesus' example inspires us to extend grace and mercy to others, even when it is difficult. By following His example, we learn to forgive freely and fully, trusting God's justice and love.

Prayer:

Heavenly Father, help me to learn from Jesus' example of forgiveness. Teach me to forgive others, even when it is hard, and to trust in Your justice and love. Amen.

NOVEMBER 26

Building a Forgiving Attitude

Bible Verse:

"Blessed are the merciful, for they will be shown mercy." — Matthew 5:7 (MSG)

Commentary:

Building a forgiving attitude involves cultivating a heart that is quick to forgive and slow to hold grudges. Matthew 5:7 highlights the blessing of being merciful, promising that those who show mercy will receive it in return. A forgiving attitude reflects God's love and grace, allowing us to live in harmony with others. By choosing to forgive quickly and completely, we prevent resentment from taking root in our hearts. A forgiving attitude promotes healing, peace, and unity in our relationships and our own hearts.

Prayer:

Lord, help me to build a forgiving attitude and to be quick to forgive others. Teach me to show mercy and to reflect Your love and grace in my relationships. Amen.

Transforming Pain into Purpose

Bible Verse:

"And we know that in all things God works for the good of those who love him, who have been called according to his purpose." — Romans 8:28 (MSG)

Commentary:

Transforming pain into purpose involves trusting that God can use our struggles for good. Romans 8:28 assures us that God works in all things for the good of those who love Him, turning our pain into purpose. When we choose to forgive and release our hurts to God, He can use them to reinforce us and help others. By sharing our stories of healing and forgiveness, we encourage others and bring glory to God. Transforming pain into purpose allows us to find meaning in our suffering and to grow in faith and resilience.

Prayer:

Heavenly Father, help me to transform my pain into purpose and to trust in Your plan for my life. Teach me to use my experiences to strengthen others and to bring glory to Your name. Amen.

NOVEMBER 28

Finding Strength in Forgiveness

Bible Verse:

"I can do all this through him who gives me strength." — Philippians 4:13 (MSG)

Commentary:

Finding strength in forgiveness involves relying on God's power to help us forgive and heal. Philippians 4:13 reminds us that we can do all things through Christ, who gives us strength. Forgiving others, and even ourselves, can be challenging, especially when the hurt is deep. By depending on God's strength, we find the courage and ability to forgive. Forgiveness empowers us to let go of the past and embrace the future with hope and trust in God's grace.

Prayer:

Lord, help me to find strength in forgiveness and to rely on Your power to heal and restore. Teach me to forgive, even when it is difficult, trusting in Your strength and grace. Amen.

NOVEMBER 29

Reflecting on Your Healing Progress

Bible Verse:

"Praise the Lord, my soul, and forget not all his benefits—who forgives all your sins and heals all your diseases." — Psalm 103:2-3 (MSG)

Commentary:

Reflecting on your healing progress involves looking back at the journey you have taken and recognizing God's work in your life. Psalm 103:2-3 reminds us to praise the Lord and not forget all His benefits, including His forgiveness and healing. By taking time to reflect on how far you have come, you can appreciate the growth and transformation that have taken place. This reflection encourages gratitude for God's faithfulness and inspires you to continue seeking His healing and grace.

Prayer:

Heavenly Father, help me to reflect on my healing journey and to recognize Your work in my life. Teach me to appreciate the progress I have made and to give thanks for Your faithfulness and grace. Amen.

NOVEMBER 30

Celebrating Milestones in Healing

Bible Verse:

"Rejoice in the Lord always. I will say it again: Rejoice!" — Philippians 4:4 (MSG)

Commentary:

Celebrating milestones in healing involves acknowledging the significant moments and breakthroughs in your journey. Philippians 4:4 encourages us to rejoice in the Lord always, highlighting the importance of celebrating our progress. By recognizing and celebrating these milestones, we affirm the work God has done in our lives and build confidence in His continued guidance. Celebrating healing milestones also inspires hope and encourages perseverance, reminding us that every step forward is worth rejoicing over.

Prayer:

Lord, help me to celebrate the milestones in my healing journey and to rejoice in Your work in my life. Teach me to recognize the significant moments of growth and to give thanks for Your guidance and love. Amen.

WELCOME TO THE MONTH OF DECEMBER – THEME: INTEGRATION AND REFLECTION

DECEMBER 1

The Year in Review

Bible Verse:

"Teach us to number our days, that we may gain a heart of wisdom." — Psalm 90:12 (MSG)

Commentary:

The year in review involves taking a comprehensive look back at the past twelve months, reflecting on all that has happened. Psalm 90:12 reminds us to be mindful of our time and to seek wisdom from our experiences. By reviewing the year, we can acknowledge both the joys and the sorrows, recognizing how they have contributed to our growth. This reflection allows us to see the hand of God in our journey, helping us appreciate the lessons learned and the ways we have changed.

Prayer:

Heavenly Father, help me to look back on this year with a heart of wisdom. Teach me to see Your hand in all that has happened and to grow from each experience. Amen.

DECEMBER 2

Lessons Learned

Bible Verse:

"Your word is a lamp for my feet, a light on my path."
— Psalm 119:105 (MSG)

Commentary:

Reflecting on the lessons learned throughout the year is a vital part of personal and spiritual growth. Psalm 119:105 emphasizes that God's Word is a guide, providing light for our path. By considering the lessons we've learned, we can understand how God has guided and directed us through various experiences. These lessons often come through challenges and triumphs alike, shaping us and refining our character. Embracing these insights helps us grow wiser and better equipped for the future.

Prayer:

Lord, help me to reflect on the lessons I've learned this year. Teach me to value the wisdom gained from each experience and to carry these lessons into the future. Amen.

DECEMBER 3

Celebrating Achievements

Bible Verse:

"Rejoice in the Lord always. I will say it again: Rejoice!" — Philippians 4:4 (MSG)

Commentary:

Celebrating achievements is an important aspect of acknowledging God's blessings and recognizing our efforts. Philippians 4:4 encourages us to rejoice in the Lord always, reminding us to celebrate the good things in life. Reflecting on our accomplishments allows us to see the progress we've made and to be grateful for God's guidance and strength. Rejoicing these milestones helps us build confidence in our abilities and motivates us to continue pursuing our goals with faith and determination.

Prayer:

Heavenly Father, help me to celebrate the achievements of this year and to rejoice in Your goodness. Teach me to recognize the progress I've made and to be thankful for Your guidance and strength. Amen.

DECEMBER 4

Recognizing Challenges

Bible Verse:

"Consider it pure joy, my brothers and sisters, whenever you face trials of many kinds." — James 1:2 (MSG)

Commentary:

Recognizing challenges is a crucial step in understanding how they have shaped us and contributed to our growth. James 1:2 encourages us to consider it pure joy when facing trials, knowing that these experiences test our faith and build perseverance. By reflecting on the challenges we faced this year, we can appreciate how they have strengthened us and taught us valuable lessons. Recognizing these difficult moments helps us see God's faithfulness and resilience at work in our lives.

Prayer:

Lord, help me to recognize the challenges I faced this year and to find joy in the growth they brought. Teach me to appreciate the strength and perseverance I gained through these experiences. Amen.

DECEMBER 5

Embracing Change

Bible Verse:

"There is a time for everything and a season for every activity under the heavens." — Ecclesiastes 3:1 (MSG)

Commentary:

Embracing change involves recognizing that life is full of seasons and that each brings its own set of challenges and blessings. Ecclesiastes 3:1 reminds us that there is a time for everything, highlighting the inevitability of change. Reflecting on how change has impacted our year helps us understand its role in our growth and development. Embracing change allows us to adapt, grow, and learn, trusting that God is guiding us through each new season.

Prayer:

Heavenly Father, help me to embrace the changes I experienced this year and to trust in Your plan for my life. Teach me to see each season as an opportunity for growth and learning. Amen.

DECEMBER 6

Gratitude for the Journey

Bible Verse:

"Give thanks in all circumstances; for this is God's will for you in Christ Jesus." — 1 Thessalonians 5:18 (MSG)

Commentary:

Gratitude for the journey involves expressing thankfulness for all the experiences, both good and bad, that have shaped us this year. 1 Thessalonians 5:18 instructs us to give thanks in all circumstances, recognizing that each moment is part of God's plan. By cultivating thankfulness for the journey, we can appreciate the growth and transformation that have occurred. This gratitude helps us maintain a positive outlook and trust in God's purpose for our lives, even when the path is challenging.

Prayer:

Lord, help me to be grateful for the journey I've been on this year. Teach me to give thanks in all circumstances and to trust in Your plan for my life. Amen.

DECEMBER 7

Evaluating Your Spiritual Growth

Bible Verse:

"But grow in the grace and knowledge of our Lord and Savior Jesus Christ. To him be glory both now and forever! Amen." — 2 Peter 3:18 (MSG)

Commentary:

Evaluating your spiritual growth is an important part of reflecting on the past year and preparing for the future. 2 Peter 3:18 encourages us to grow in grace and knowledge of Jesus Christ, reminding us of the importance of continual spiritual development. By assessing how our relationship with God has deepened, we can identify areas where we have grown and areas where we need further growth. This reflection helps us set spiritual goals for the new year and remain committed to our journey with God.

Prayer:

Heavenly Father, help me to evaluate my spiritual growth over the past year. Teach me to grow in grace and knowledge of You and to remain committed to my journey with You. Amen.

DECEMBER 8

Applying Lessons to Daily Life

Bible Verse:

"Do not merely listen to the word, and so deceive yourselves. Do what it says." — James 1:22 (MSG)

Commentary:

Applying lessons to daily life means taking what we've learned throughout the year and putting it into practice. James 1:22 encourages us not just to listen to the word but to act on it. By integrating the insights and wisdom we've gained, we can transform our daily actions and decisions. This application helps solidify our growth, ensuring that the lessons we've learned become a part of who we are and how we live. It's through action that true transformation takes place.

Prayer:

Lord, help me to apply the lessons I've learned this year to my daily life. Teach me to not just hear Your word but to live it out each DAY. Amen.

DECEMBER 9

Practicing Patience

Bible Verse:

"Be completely humble and gentle; be patient, bearing with one another in love." — Ephesians 4:2 (MSG)

Commentary:

Practicing patience is essential for maintaining peace and fostering healthy relationships. Ephesians 4:2 calls us to be humble, gentle, and patient, bearing with one another in love. Patience allows us to navigate life's challenges with grace and understanding. It helps us respond to circumstances calmly and with empathy, preventing conflict and promoting harmony. By practicing patience, we reflect God's love and demonstrate our growth in character and maturity.

Prayer:

Heavenly Father, help me to practice patience in my daily life. Teach me to be humble, gentle, and understanding, reflecting Your love in all my interactions. Amen.

DECEMBER 10

Strengthening Faith

Bible Verse:

"Now faith is confidence in what we hope for and assurance about what we do not see." — Hebrews 11:1 (MSG)

Commentary:

Strengthening faith involves deepening our trust in God, even when we cannot see the outcome. Hebrews 11:1 defines faith as confidence in what we hope for and assurance about what we do not see. By reflecting on the past year, we can identify moments where our faith was challenged and strengthened. Building a stronger faith requires consistent prayer, reading Scripture, and trusting God's promises. As we continue to rely on Him, our faith becomes more robust, guiding us through life's uncertainties with confidence.

Prayer:

Lord, help me to strengthen my faith and to trust in You more deeply. Teach me to have confidence in Your promises and to rely on You in all circumstances. Amen.

DECEMBER 11

Living with Purpose

Bible Verse:

"For I know the plans I have for you," declares the Lord, "plans to prosper you and not to harm you, plans to give you hope and a future." — Jeremiah 29:11 (MSG)

Commentary:

Living with purpose means aligning our actions with God's plan for our lives. Jeremiah 29:11 reassures us that God has plans for us—plans for hope and a future. By reflecting on what gives our lives meaning, we can better understand our purpose and make choices that align with it. Living intentionally and with purpose and resolution helps us stay focused on what truly matters, guiding our decisions and actions toward fulfilling God's calling for us.

Prayer:

Heavenly Father, help me to live with purpose and to align my actions with Your plan for my life. Teach me to trust in Your promises and to pursue the path You have set before me. Amen.

DECEMBER 12

Developing Resilience

Bible Verse:

"Not only so, but we also glory in our sufferings, because we know that suffering produces perseverance; perseverance, character; and character, hope." — Romans 5:3-4 (MSG)

Commentary:

Developing resilience involves learning to endure hardships with a spirit of hope and perseverance. Romans 5:3-4 teaches that suffering produces perseverance, which in turn builds character and leads to hope. Reflecting on the trials we have faced this year, we can see how they have helped us grow stronger and more resilient. Building resilience means trusting in God's strength, remaining steadfast in faith, and viewing challenges as opportunities for growth.

Prayer:

Lord, help me to develop resilience and to persevere through trials with hope. Teach me to trust in Your strength and to see challenges as opportunities for growth and character-building. Amen.

DECEMBER 13

Fostering Positive Relationships

Bible Verse:

"A friend loves at all times, and a brother is born for a time of adversity." — Proverbs 17:17 (MSG)

Commentary:

Fostering positive relationships involves investing in the people who love, uplift, and support us. Proverbs 17:17 reminds us that a friend loves at all times, and a brother is born for adversity. Reflecting on our relationships over the past year, we can identify those who have been a source of encouragement and strength. By nurturing these connections, we build a supportive network that enhances our well-being and spiritual growth. Strong, positive relationships are vital for a fulfilling and meaningful life.

Prayer:

Heavenly Father, help me to foster positive relationships and to invest in those who uplift and support me. Teach me to be a loving and faithful friend, reflecting Your love in all my interactions. Amen.

DECEMBER 14

Incorporating Healthy Habits

Bible Verse:

"Do you not know that your bodies are temples of the Holy Spirit, who is in you, whom you have received from God? You are not your own." — 1 Corinthians 6:19 (MSG)

Commentary:

Incorporating healthy habits is essential for nurturing our physical, emotional, and spiritual well-being. 1 Corinthians 6:19 reminds us that our bodies are temples of the Holy Spirit, and we are called to honor God with our bodies. Reflecting on the habits we've developed over the past year, we can identify which ones have contributed positively to our health and well-being. By committing to maintaining and building on these healthy habits, we honor God and support our overall growth.

Prayer:

Lord, help me to incorporate healthy habits into my daily life. Teach me to honor my body as a temple of the Holy Spirit and to nurture my physical, emotional, and spiritual well-being. Amen.

Setting New Goals

Bible Verse:

"Commit to the Lord whatever you do, and he will establish your plans." — Proverbs 16:3 (MSG)

Commentary:

Setting new goals involves prayerfully considering what you want to achieve in the upcoming year and aligning your desires with God's will. Proverbs 16:3 encourages us to commit our plans to the Lord, assuring us that He will help establish them. By setting clear, meaningful goals, you create a roadmap for personal and spiritual growth. These goals should reflect your values, aspirations, and God's purpose for your life, guiding you toward fulfilling His will in the coming year.

Prayer:

Heavenly Father, help me to set new goals that align with Your will for my life. Teach me to commit my plans to You and to trust that You will establish them according to Your purpose. Amen.

DECEMBER 16

Creating a Vision Board

Bible Verse:

"Where there is no vision, the people perish." — Proverbs 29:18 (MSG)

Commentary:

Creating a vision board is a creative way to visualize your aspirations and keep your goals in front of you throughout the year. Proverbs 29:18 emphasizes the importance of vision in guiding our lives. By compiling images, scriptures, and words that represent your hopes and dreams, you create a tangible reminder of what you are working towards. A vision board serves as daily motivation and helps you remain focused on your spiritual journey as well as your personal growth.

Prayer:

Lord, help me to create a vision for the new year that reflects Your will for my life. Teach me to stay focused on my goals and to pursue them with passion and purpose. Amen.

Reevaluating Priorities

Bible Verse:

"But seek first his kingdom and his righteousness, and all these things will be given to you as well." — Matthew 6:33 (MSG)

Commentary:

Reevaluating priorities involves taking a step back to assess what truly matters in your life and ensuring that your actions align with those values. Matthew 6:33 reminds us to seek first God's kingdom and righteousness, promising that everything else will fall into place. By reassessing your priorities, you can make sure that your time and energy are focused on what's most important—your relationship with God, your family, and your personal growth.

Prayer:

Heavenly Father, help me to reevaluate my priorities and to seek first Your kingdom and righteousness. Teach me to focus on what truly matters and to align my actions with Your will. Amen.

Planning for Continued Growth

Bible Verse:

"Let us run with perseverance the race marked out for us, fixing our eyes on Jesus, the pioneer, and perfecter of faith." — Hebrews 12:1-2 (MSG)

Commentary:

Planning for continued growth involves setting a course for ongoing development in all areas of your life. Hebrews 12:1-2 encourages us to run with perseverance the race set before us, keeping our focus on Jesus. By identifying specific areas where you want to grow—whether spiritually, emotionally, or physically—you can create a plan to help you stay on track. This intentional planning ensures that you are always moving forward, continually seeking to become the person God created you to be.

Prayer:

Lord, help me to plan for continued growth in the new year. Teach me to run with perseverance and to keep my eyes fixed on Jesus, the pioneer and perfecter of my faith. Amen.

DECEMBER 19

Embracing New Opportunities

Bible Verse:

"Here I am! I stand at the door and knock. If anyone hears my voice and opens the door, I will come in and eat with that person, and they with me." — Revelation 3:20 (MSG)

Commentary:

Embracing new opportunities involves being open to the doors God may open for you in the coming year. Revelation 3:20 depicts Jesus standing at the door and knocking, inviting us to welcome Him into our lives. By staying attuned to God's voice and being willing to step out in faith, you can embrace new challenges and opportunities that align with His purpose for you. Being open to new possibilities can lead to growth, fulfillment, and a deeper and more profound relationship with God.

Prayer:

Heavenly Father, help me to embrace new opportunities in the coming year. Teach me to listen for Your voice and to step out in faith when You open doors for me. Amen.

DECEMBER 20

Cultivating a Positive Mindset

Bible Verse:

"Finally, brothers and sisters, whatever is true, whatever is noble, whatever is right, whatever is pure, whatever is lovely, whatever is admirable—if anything is excellent or praiseworthy—think about such things." — Philippians 4:8 (MSG)

Commentary:

Cultivating a positive mindset involves focusing on what is good, true, and uplifting, even in challenging circumstances. Philippians 4:8 encourages us to think about things that are excellent or praiseworthy, guiding our minds toward positivity and hope. By intentionally choosing to dwell on positive thoughts and trusting in God's goodness, you can maintain a positive outlook, regardless of what comes your way. This mindset helps you stay grounded in faith and ready to face whatever challenges the new year may bring.

Prayer:

Lord, help me to cultivate a positive mindset and to focus on what is good, true, and praiseworthy. Teach me to trust in Your goodness and to maintain hope in all circumstances. Amen.

Trusting God's Plan

Bible Verse:

"For I know the plans I have for you," declares the Lord, "plans to prosper you and not to harm you, plans to give you hope and a future." — Jeremiah 29:11 (MSG)

Commentary:

Trusting God's plan involves having faith that He has a purpose and direction for your life, even when the path is unclear. Jeremiah 29:11 reassures us that God's plans are for our good, to prosper us, and to give us hope. By trusting in God's sovereignty and goodness, you can face the new year with confidence, knowing that He is in control. This trust helps you navigate uncertainties with peace, knowing that God's plans are always for your ultimate benefit and growth.

Prayer:

Heavenly Father, help me to trust in Your plan for my life and to have faith in Your promises. Teach me to rely on Your wisdom and to find peace in Your sovereignty. Amen.

DECEMBER 22

Enhancing Your Prayer Life

Bible Verse:

"Devote yourselves to prayer, being watchful and thankful." — Colossians 4:2 (MSG)

Commentary:

Enhancing your prayer life involves deepening your connection with God through consistent, heartfelt communication. Colossians 4:2 encourages us to be devoted to prayer, highlighting the importance of being watchful and thankful. By setting aside intentional time each DAY to pray, you can strengthen your relationship with God and gain clarity and peace in your daily life. Focusing on gratitude during prayer also helps cultivate a thankful heart, reminding you of God's blessings and faithfulness.

Prayer:

Heavenly Father, help me to enhance my prayer life and to devote myself to consistent, heartfelt communication with You. Teach me to be watchful and thankful, deepening my relationship with You through prayer. Amen.

Engaging in Scripture

Bible Verse:

"All Scripture is God-breathed and is useful for teaching, rebuking, correcting and training in righteousness." — 2 Timothy 3:16 (MSG)

Commentary:

Engaging in Scripture involves regularly reading and meditating on God's Word to gain wisdom, guidance, and strength. 2 Timothy 3:16 reminds us that all Scripture is inspired by God and valuable for our spiritual growth. By dedicating time to studying the Bible, you allow God's truth to shape your thoughts and actions, guiding you on the path of righteousness. Engaging with Scripture daily helps you stay rooted in faith and better equipped to handle life's challenges.

Prayer:

Lord, help me to absorb more deeply in Your Word and to seek wisdom and guidance through Scripture. Teach me to value the Bible as a source of truth and strength in my spiritual journey. Amen.

DECEMBER 24

Seeking Fellowship

Bible Verse:

"And let us consider how we may spur one another on toward love and good deeds, not giving up meeting together, as some are in the habit of doing but encouraging one another." — Hebrews 10:24-25 (MSG)

Commentary:

Seeking fellowship involves actively participating in a community of believers to encourage one another and grow together in faith. Hebrews 10:24-25 emphasizes the importance of meeting together and encouraging one another in love and good deeds. By engaging in fellowship, you find support, accountability, and encouragement, which are vital for spiritual growth. Being part of a faith community helps you stay connected to God and others, fostering a sense of belonging and mutual edification.

Prayer:

Heavenly Father, help me to seek fellowship with other believers and to actively participate in a faith community. Teach me to encourage others and to grow together in love and good deeds. Amen.

Serving Others

Bible Verse:

"For even the Son of Man did not come to be served, but to serve, and to give his life as a ransom for many." — Mark 10:45 (MSG)

Commentary:

Serving others involves following Jesus' example of selflessness and humility by meeting the needs of those around you. Mark 10:45 reminds us that Jesus came not to be served but to serve, setting a model for us to follow. By serving others, you demonstrate God's love in action and fulfill His call to love your neighbor as yourself. Serving is a powerful way to grow spiritually, as it shifts your focus from yourself to others and helps you cultivate a heart of compassion and generosity.

Prayer:

Lord, help me to serve others with a heart of humility and love. Teach me to follow Jesus' example and to demonstrate Your love through my actions. Amen.

DECEMBER 26

Expanding Your Spiritual Knowledge

Bible Verse:

"The heart of the discerning acquires knowledge, for the ears of the wise seek it out." — Proverbs 18:15 (MSG)

Commentary:

Expanding your spiritual knowledge involves seeking to learn more about your faith and deepening your understanding of God's Word. Proverbs 18:15 highlights the value of acquiring knowledge and seeking wisdom. By studying theology, attending Bible studies, or reading Christian books, you can expand your understanding of God's character and His will for your life. This knowledge helps strengthen your faith, equipping you to live a life that honors God and reflects His truth.

Prayer:

Heavenly Father, help me to magnify my spiritual knowledge and to seek wisdom and understanding in my faith journey. Teach me to value learning and to grow in my knowledge of You and Your Word. Amen.

Reflecting on God's Faithfulness

Bible Verse:

"The steadfast love of the Lord never ceases; his mercies never come to an end; they are new every morning; great is your faithfulness." — Lamentations 3:22-23 (MSG)

Commentary:

Reflecting on God's faithfulness involves remembering the ways He has been faithful to you throughout the year and expressing gratitude for His unwavering love and mercy. Lamentations 3:22-23 remind us that God's steadfast love never ceases, and His mercies are new every morning. By taking time to reflect on God's faithfulness, you can strengthen your trust in Him and renew your commitment to follow His will. This reflection encourages a grateful heart and a deeper understanding of God's character.

Prayer:

Heavenly Father, help me to reflect on Your faithfulness and to remember the ways You have been with me this year. Teach me to trust in Your steadfast love and to be grateful for Your mercy and grace. Amen.

DECEMBER 28

Anticipating the Future

Bible Verse:

"For I know the plans I have for you," declares the Lord, "plans to prosper you and not to harm you, plans to give you hope and a future." — Jeremiah 29:11 (MSG)

Commentary:

Anticipating the future involves looking forward with hope and confidence in God's plans for your life. Jeremiah 29:11 reminds us that God has plans to prosper us and give us hope and a future. As you reflect on the past year and prepare for the new one, trust that God is working in every detail of your life. By placing your hope in His promises, you can face the future with optimism and assurance, knowing that He is guiding your path and has good things in store for you.

Prayer:

Heavenly Father, help me to anticipate the future with hope and confidence in Your plans. Teach me to trust in Your promises and to look forward with faith in Your guidance and love. Amen.

Setting Intentions for the New Year

Bible Verse:

"But seek first his kingdom and his righteousness, and all these things will be given to you as well." — Matthew 6:33 (MSG)

Commentary:

Setting intentions for the new year involves focusing on what truly matters and aligning your goals with God's will. Matthew 6:33 encourages us to seek first God's kingdom and righteousness, promising that everything else will be provided. As you set your intentions for the year ahead, prioritize your spiritual growth and your relationship with God. By focusing on His kingdom and righteousness, you can ensure that your goals and desires are aligned with His purpose, leading to a fulfilling and blessed year.

Prayer:

Lord, help me to set intentions for the new year that align with Your will. Teach me to seek first Your kingdom and righteousness and to trust that You will provide for all my needs. Amen.

DECEMBER 30

Committing to Your Spiritual Path

Bible Verse:

"Trust in the Lord with all your heart and lean not on your own understanding; in all your ways submit to him, and he will make your paths straight." — Proverbs 3:5-6 (MSG)

Commentary:

Committing to your spiritual path involves dedicating yourself to a journey of continuous growth and deepening your relationship with God. Proverbs 3:5-6 encourages us to trust in the Lord with all our heart and to submit to Him in all our ways, promising that He will guide our paths. By committing to your spiritual path, you demonstrate your conviction in God's plan and your desire to grow closer to Him. This commitment helps you stay focused on what truly matters and encourages you to pursue God's will with all your heart.

Prayer:

Heavenly Father, help me to commit to my spiritual path and to trust in Your guidance. Teach me to lean on You and to follow Your will with all my heart. Amen.

DECEMBER 31

Embracing New Beginnings

Bible Verse:

"Therefore, if anyone is in Christ, the new creation has come: The old has gone, the new is here!" — 2 Corinthians 5:17 (MSG)

Commentary:

Embracing new beginnings involves letting go of the past and stepping into the new opportunities that God provides. 2 Corinthians 5:17 reminds us that in Christ, we are a new creation; the old has gone, and the new is here. As you move into the new year, be willing to release past mistakes, regrets, or hurts and embrace the fresh start God offers. By focusing on the new creation you are in Christ, you can approach each DAY with hope and expectation for what God has in store.

Prayer:

Lord, help me to embrace new beginnings and to let go of the past. Teach me to see each DAY as a fresh start in You and to walk confidently into the future You have prepared for me. Amen.

ABOUT THE AUTHOR

After dedicating over 20 years to teaching and empowerment ministries, Lyn had a powerful revelation. Despite her extensive knowledge of the Word, she realized she wasn't living the transformed life God intended for her. Struggling with an ordinary and mundane lifestyle, she hadn't fully embraced God's promises as taught in the Scriptures. With renewed passion, she decided to take a fresh approach to the Word, seeking God through it in a unique way. This experience proved to be liberating and profoundly enlightening, bringing new insights into familiar verses and reigniting her faith. Diligently documenting her divine encounters in a journal, along with the devotions and inspirations that brought clarity and meaning to her busy life, allowed her to witness God's intricate plans for an abundance-filled life every day. Through daily devotion to God and His Word, she unlocked the key to experiencing a rich and fulfilling life, understanding that God's desire for her is to embrace a life that is continuously renewed and transformed.